RABINDRANATH TAGORE : A QUEST

RABINDRANATH TAGORE : A QUEST

MOHIT CHAKRABARTI

GYAN

GYAN PUBLISHING HOUSE

New Delhi 110 002

RABINDRANATH TAGORE : A QUEST
(*BIOGRAPHy, Literature, Culture*)

ISBN : 81-212-0491-7
Library of Congress Card No. 93-900332

Published 1995 in India by
Gyan Publishing House
5, Ansari Road
New Delhi-110 002

Laser typeset at DRO Phototypesetter, Delhi and printed at Mehra Offset Press, New Delh-110 022

Dedicated to
Professor R.P. Sharma,
University of delhi
&
Dr. Martin Kämpchen,
Santiniketan.

PREFACE

Re-thinking Rabindranath Tagore is re-thinking humanity. The quest for the essence of his multi-dimensional genius is the quest unending. It is a quest for the Innermost one with all devotion to Truth. Goodness and Beauty. "The Quest for the Innermost One" is an introspective study of appreciating Rabindranath Tagore from this end in view.

Creativity, an eternal mystery in man, affords a new meaning in terms of talent and excellence. Education for creativity enjoys a ukase not because there is an absence of awareness in the arena of learning but essentially because it is not endearingly synchronized with the exercise of freedom and joy. "Education for creativity and Talent : Tagoreian perspectives" is an endeavour to spell out Tagorean viewpoints intensively.

The songs of Rabindranath Tagore are the perennial treasures of a creative artist *par excellence. His songs of love in particular are incomparable and unparalleled manifestations of the finer nuances of love that glorify mankind.* "The Love Songs of Rabindranath Tagore " is an humble attempt to expose this fact.

That Tagore is more aware of mass education than most of the celebrated protagonists rest assured with theoretical ideas can be reassessed by "Mass Education : Tagorean Guidelines".

"The Mystic Vision of Tagore in *Gitanjali"* and "The Concept of Transcendence in Tagore's Folk Songs" may amply contribute to the quest for the essence of Tagore. Again, "Farewell to Earth : Tagore's Vision of Death" and "Interpreting Tagore's *Janmadine*" may reveal newer avenues of Tagorean philosophy of life and death.

Civilization, a birth-right of mankind, is even now in the meleé of macabre confusion. To Tagore, the crisis of civilization that has caused untold mental unrest for a foreseeable doom in utter passivity and destruction necessitates a re-appraisal right now or never. "Tagore's 'Crisis in Civilization' : A Re-

Thinking" may evoke ardent response from every revered reader.

I gratefully recall the love, affection and serene scholarship of Professor R.P. Sharma, University of Delhi and Dr. Martin Kämpchen, an eminent German Scholar in Tagore studies. I dedicate my book to them as a token of my reverence.

If the book—a quest unending in the world of Tagore—pleases the revered readers and promotes a new sense of consciousness in Tagoreana, I would consider my labour lavishly rewarded.

(Mohit Chakrabarti)

Seemantika

Seemanto Palli

SANTINIKETAN - 731235

West Bengal

India.

CONTENTS

CONTENTS

THE QUEST FOR THE INNERMOST ONE

To be conscious is to be prepared within and to be prepared within is to be ready for the advent of the Innermost One. A quest unending, the search goes on with excellence encountering better excellence. The 'I' within wants to be liberated from every ukase consequential to all shortcomings and adverse experiences. Perhaps these are badly needed, for who denies imperfections disallowing entrance to the door of deliverance ? The perfumes of promises are yet to be inhaled. The poignance of perfection is yet to be apprehended and accordingly, appreciated. 'What act', as Browning observes, 'proved all its thoughts had been ?' notwithstanding. And so, the I within every individual more or less cannot but be restless through ceaseless endeavour in the selfstyled cocoon of consciousness. Is the Innermost One far away from the reach of human consciousness ? What are the avenues of meeting Him ? How does He marvel at the excellence where He is existent ? How can His marvels be identified and appreciated ? When does he expose himself in the best of brilliance and magnificence ? Where does he want to chant the embodiment to be attuned to or synchronized, and how ? All these and a host of other graver queries hover round the little I like constellations of stars to be hallowed with the promise of better poignance of perfection in the quest for the innermost One.

Unlike any other appreciator and apostle of creative consciousness, Rabindranath Tagore endeavours to pave avenues of inward vision through a certain sense of unbiased adoration for the unending vastness in and around himself. The universe as the great exponent of *ananda* and *amrita,* Joy and nectar, does not avert his inward vision. The success of life is, indeed, evaluated in the yardstick of experience encountered and transgrafted for the unity blessed with greatness of truth exposed everywhere. Tagore's own appreciation serves a better guideline :

In sorrows, bereavements and agonies of life
A message of the saint has day by day been brighter in my mind—
The universe manifests itself in the forms of joy and nectar
Whate'er is little thro' opposed evidence
Does show its easy skill in dwarfing the great.
One who encounters the grandeur of Truth
Spread over space and time unending,
In the form of the undivisible,
Glorious has his life become in this world.

— Rabindranath Tagore : *Rogashajyay, Rabindra-Rachanavali,* Vol. III, No. 25, Government of West Bengal, Calcutta, 1983, p. 804.

[Translated by Author]

The quest for the formless and colourless, *sans* day or night and for the wordless in the midst of the all Beautiful is, as Tagore introspects, undeniably thrilling. The rest of the nuances of inward excellence blessed with the incomparable love of the Infinite amid the hallowed beauty of the morning and the evening in the vast expanse of the sky brings forth a sombre quietude, a readiness for the soul to have an exciting flight for deliverance. Is the way to inwardness not a way for self-purification—'The stainless white radiance' of everlasting purity ? Why not listen to the song of the poet ?

Thou art the sky and thou art the nest as well.

O thou beautiful, there in the nest it is thy love that encloses the soul with colours and sounds and odours.

There comes the morning with the golden basket in her right hand bearing the wreath of beauty, silently to crown the earth.

And there comes the evening over the lonely meadows deserted by herds, through trackless paths, carrying cool draughts of peace in her golden pitcher from the western ocean of rest.

But there, where spreads the infinite sky for the soul to take her flight in, reigns the stainless white radiance. There is no day or night, nor form nor colour, and never, never a word.

— Rabindranath Tagore : *Gitanjali,* Macmillan Pocket Tagore Edition. Macmillan India Limited, 1981, LXVII, p. 45

Life with all limitations and inconsistencies awaits cohesion in the inward vision of the All Beautiful. The creative sensibilities fillip it endlessly to be in unison with the Innermost One. The triumph of human endeavour whatsoever or howsoever only indicates the agonies of the soul within—the agonies that prize one with vain pride and futility only to be renewed in crystallized consciousness. The real I, therefore, cannot help rejecting all so-called achievements and protections that betray the vision of the Illumined One. The only quality that thrives and heightens human sensibilities is unalloyed love for mankind. Love alone can pave the surest and most enviable avenue for the great journey to the Innermost One. It alone can defy death and teach the lesson of immortality of mankind. Tagore makes a categorical statement when he courageously asserts the great truth of love as an indomitable and eternal force of the existence of man for time beyond time.

I do not have faith in my achievements
Know I that the sea of time
With strokes of waves all the time
Would wipe it away day by day.

Myself do I believe
Filling that cup day and night
The eternal juice of this universe
Have I drunk.

The love of every moment
Amid it has been stored
The burden of sorrow tattered it not
Nor dust blackened
Its artistry.

Know I that when I would bid farewell
To the battle stage of the world
The forest of flower would at every season give evidence
That I have loved this universe.

This love alone is truth—a gift of this life.
At the time of bidding farewell
This truth untarnished would defy death.

— Rabindranath Tagore : *Rogashajyay; Rabindra-Rachanavali*, Government of West Bengal, Calcutta, 1983, Vol III, No. 26, p. 805.

[Translated by Author.]

The reminiscence of love for this world as the poet feels within will present him all the while with the saga of poignance that will ultimately reward him with perfection. All inconsistencies will be swept away with the surging waves of the song of renewed consciousness. All visions of the Innermost One will be hallowed with the lustre of brilliance baked in the fire of experience. The muse of the poet becomes our very own for it also reveals our own untold agonies :

My mind admits not to account for what I did not receive.

In the shadow and light of the heart today on the
flute has been played

This world did I love and that reminiscence
To the mind returns time and again

With the southern wind in the endless spring
Has my own basket filled.

Tears deep and dense in the core of the heart exist,

In the saga of pain turn meditation a success in the
mist.

Now and then the strings were of course torn apart,
but who wails for that ?

And yet the tune came again and again and that do
I remember today.

— Rabindranath Tagore : *'Gaan'*, *'Rabindra-Rachanavali'*, Government of West Bengal, Calcutta, 1987, Vol. IV, No. 1412, p. 545.

[Translated by Author.]

For unison with the Great I that opens out the auspicious gateway of consciousness, Tagore finds a great point of similarity between the inward joy and the soul that is nursled and enkindled with purity of perfection. There can, therefore, be no alternative but to enter into the kingdom of joy in the diverse world of creativity to have the blessings of the Innermost One. The quest of the poet reveals the truth :

The touch of joy that in the heart of light I receive

Know I that my soul no difference does conceive

From an ancient, lustrous source

On the forehead, initiated have I been,

The mark of victory was given

The nectar do I possess, it has informed that

I can be united with the Great

In this world of diversity
In the avenue of joy may I have an entry.

— Rabindranath Tagore : *Arogya (Convalescence), Rabindra-Rachanavali,* Government of West Bengal, Calcutta, Vol. III, No. 32, p. 839.

[Translated by Author.]

The preparation of mankind for emergence of consciousness pure and serene is the only way to be in unison with the Innermost One. Tagore, therefore, continually tries to shatter all enchantments of the Little I in order to have the glorious light of consciousness. Let all falsehood be eliminated by embracing the vast expansion of eternity—the Truth Eternal. Let every life be mused with the harmony of inner vastness. Let the light of Truth be enkindled in the soul within. Let the mind be invigorated with the freshness of life in beauty and joy. In the words of Tagore :

Let the cocoon of this life unmask
The bright halo of consciousness
Express the eternal form of truth
By piercing the mist
Let the light of joy of a Man Eternal
Amid all men
Be enkindled in my mind
Beyond the silent world of worldly grievance
Let me behold the blessed form of the Eternal.
Whatever is amply meaningless and critical in this life,
Whatever embodies falsehood in the sham value of the society
Leaving aside all beggarly and
Troubled crowd
Let me know the true meaning with my vivid eyes—
Prior to crossing the bar.

— Rabindranath Tagore : *Arogya (Convalescence), Rabindra-Rachanavali,* Government of West Bengal, Calcutta, 1983, Vol. III, No. 33, p. 840.

Emancipation from the little I in communion with the king of kings by means of love is the only avenue of perfection of life. Life illuminated with this conscious approach to mutual love between the Lord of all heavens and man washes away all dirt and dualities, ambiguities and vicissitudes of human thoughts and sensibilities. The affluence of life in the form of accumulated wealth of love pure and serene also ensures the will of the king of kings because life then merges in the will of the Endless. Tagore crystallizes this aspect of the fusion of love in man and the king of kings very adroitly :

> Thus it is that the joy in me is so full.
>
> Thus it is that thou hast come down to me.
>
> O Thou Lord of all heavens, where would
>
> be thy love if I were not ?
>
> Thou hast taken me as thy partner of all this wealth. In my heart is the endless play of thy delight. In my life thy will is ever taking shape.
>
> And for this, thou who art the king of kings hast decked thyself in beauty to captivate my heart. And for this thy love loses itself in the love of thy lover, and there art thou seen in the perfect union of two.
>
> — Rabindranath Tagore : *Gitanjali,* Macmillan Pocket Tagore Edition, Macmillan India Limited, 1981, No. LVI, p. 37.

Love illumined between the Lord and man is love intensified for the vision of the Innermost One. The play of love in poignance of perfection goes on until the king of kings is in fusion with love of man. It is an endless striving for which the urge for creating anew and looking upon the Innermost One as the only image of man as a perfect being goes on forever.

The doors and windows of inner consciousness for a beyonding of bare existence and inconsistencies are wide open with the prayer of self-purification. Tagore portrays the picture of human renunciation in an incomparable pattern of humble submission :

More, my lord, more
Prize me with punishment with greater furore
I remain in seclusion, I run away quite apart
Exposed have I been, can I any more my-self avert
Take away all whatever have I in store.
Do whatsoever now for my cure
Let me be the loser or let defeat come at our door
In market-places, steppings and banks do I stay
My time has waned on the laughter alone and play
Let me see how you can for my eyes tears ensure.

— Rabindranath Tagore : *Songs, Rabindra-Rachanavali,* Government of West Bengal, Calcutta, 1987, Vol. II, No. 661, p. 288.

[Translated by Author.]

The message of the Innermost One in the indescribable aura of light spread over the light in every morning brings forth a new promise of prayer. A new sense of awareness and revelation guarantees the truth that all said and done are yet to confirm harmony of the message of the heart with that of the sky. The strings of unison with the All Beautiful are yet to be attuned. Tagore has a wonderful exposure of self-evaluation woven in the words of appropriate depth of vision :

In every morning do I receive the pleasing touch of light
The heavenly honour of existence.
The flow of blood is mingled with the current of lustre
The message of light sounds in silence in body and mind.
With the palms of eyes stretched wide
Upwards do I daily behold.
The first reception of life is blessed with this light
On the shore of the setting sun at the door of this light
The last prayer of my life will be submitted,
I think I speak in vain, all words are yet to be told,

The message of the heart with that of the sky
Is yet to be attuned with the perfect tuning.
The language to me has remained unknown.

— Rabindranath Tagore : *Rogashajyay, Rabindra-Rachanavali*, Government of West Bengal, Calcutta, 1983, Vol. III, No. 32 p. 808.

[Translated by Author.]

The aura of consciousness enkindled in the light of the morning brings forth vastness in void. The Innermost One appears only when the mind is liberated from the little I. The poet's exposure is rather more explicit :

Whatever did I expect with earnest eagerness
The clasp of arms around these
When removed only then
In that emancipated arena of enchantment
The consciousness that shines out,
With the morning light,
Do I behold its inseparable identity.
Void it is and empty yet it is not
The message of the saint do I, then, can conceive—
If the sky remained *sans* pleasre in full measure
The mind and the body would be motionless in the clasping of drabness
Where could there be difference between one and the other from the point of life
If there was no joy in this sky ?

— Rabindranath Tagore : *Rogashajyay, Rabindra-Rachanavali*, Government of West Bengal, Calcutta, 1983, Vol. III, No. 36, p. 810-811.

[Translated by Author.]

How to quicken the arrival of the All Beautiful in the midst of affluence in the void ? To Tagore, it is a matter of pure objectivity by means of elimination of vain glory and honour, pride and prestige, that eat up the inner vitalities of mankind.

The time for the blessings of the Innermost One is too short to be whiled away, and so he appeals :

Float away honour and pride
And bring Him near
Offer laughter drenched with tears on His feet.
O, on His feet ye offer.
The path is becoming shadowy, the sky turns dark
Flowers dry would droop down, on flows time
O, time crosses over.

— Rabindranath Tagore : *Songs, Rabindra-Rachanavali,* Government of West Bengal, Calcutta, 1987, Vol. IV, No. 664, p. 289.

[Translated by Author.]

For unison with the Innermost One, every day with its ever new brightness of light appears with the adoration of the promise of perfection anew. The heart pulsates with the thrilling beckoning of the king of kings with all His creation in the midst of Nature. One cannot, as Tagore translates into introspective vision, miss this auspicious moment of the glory of mankind :

The most beautiful
Is adorned in the holy morning
Of the bathing of light.
The unending formless
With the touchstone of infinite forms
Is creating images of appreciation
Every day
The welcome of the ever new
At the altar of the ever old,
With unison of the green and the blue firmament
The scarf of the earth
In light and shade goes a-weaving.
The heart-beat of the sky
Does throb from leaf to leaf.
The morning's necklace sparkles

From forest to forest.
The unaccountable songs of birds
Go on thanking the goddess of the affluence of life.
The touch of human love
Does bring forth the meaning of nectar in fusion
with all,
Turns the dust of the earth pleasant,
And spreads the throne for the Eternal Man
everywhere.

— Rabindranath Tagore : *Arogya (Convalescence), Rabindra-Rachanavali,* Government of West Bengal, Calcutta, 1983, Vol. III, p. 821-822.

[Translated by Author.]

The sense of dissociation with the Innermost One often makes the unison rather bleak and remote. Is this the play of the Ever Glorious ? Or does it infuse one with the added spirit of union with the Innermost One ? Here is Tagore's answer in the unparalleled pattern of muse :

I am like a remnant of a cloud of autumn uselessly roaming in the sky, O my sun ever-glorious. Thy touch has not yet melted my vapour, making me one with thy light, and thus I count months and years separated from Thee.

If this be thy wish and if this be thy play, then take this fleeting emptiness of mine, paint it with colours, gild it with gold, float it on the wanton wind and spread it in varied wonders.

And again when it shall be thy wish to end this play at night, I shall melt and vanish away in the dark, or it may be in a smile of the white morning, in a coolness of purity transparent.

— Rabindranath Tagore : *Gitanjali,* Macmillan Pocket Tagore Edition, Macmillan India Limited, 1981, L XXX, p. 53-54.

With the frank admission of total submission to the Innermost One, life becomes a worthy arena for purity and perfection in endless endeavour. Amid the creative force of the universe, the blessings of the Innermost One can be attained only when there is a genuine urge for self-understanding in the aura of the Great Light that leads one on and on. With this belief in continual excellence of oneself through creative endeavour, Tagore prays for the beyonding of death in the rich and invaluable harvest of creative consciousness placed at the altar of the All Beautiful. Let us, therefore, be partners to the Poet's inward vision :

Standing on the edge of the playground of creation
At times do I behold
The other side of darkness
Where mingled I was in the unending consciousness
of the Great Unexpressed.
At this time of the morning today the words of
saints do I recall
Unfold, O Sun, unfold the cover of light,
Let me see in the great halo of thy inmost heart
The real form of my soul.
The I that adds its breath of life in the air at the
end of the day
That ends its body in ashes.
Let it not cast its shadow on the way of journey
In disguise of Truth.
In the playing arena on earth the taste of the
nectar have I had in happiness and sorrow
From time to time,
Time and again have I visualized the Endless
behind the veil of the finite.
Understood have I that the last meaning of this
life was there
In the form of that Beautiful.
In that muse unspeakable.
When in the playhouse the doors would be wide
open

I would leave my salutation in the temple of the
earth.
Now offer those offerings of life
That are valued beyond death.

— Rabindranath Tagore : *Janmadine, Rabindra-Rachanavali,* Government of West Bengal, Calcutta, 1983, Vol. III, No. 13, p. 853.

[Translated by Author.]

With inward preparation reinforced by preparation anew for meeting the Innermost One, the play makes the poet more romantic. He becomes more hopeful, more enthusiastic, more pulsating in his endeavour creative and sombre. The unseen countenance and the voice unheard haunts him to meet the Innermost One :

The song that I came to sing remains unsung to this day. I have spent my days in stringing and in unstringing my instrument.

The time has not come true, the words have not been rightly set; only there is the agony of wishing in my heart.

The blossom has not opened; only the wind is sighing by. I have not seen his face, nor have I listened to his voice; only have I heard gentle footsteps from the road before my house.

The live long day has passed in spreading his seat on the floor; but the lamp has not been lit and I cannot ask him into my house.

I live in the hope of meeting with him; but this meeting is not yet.

— Rabindranath Tagore : *Gitanjali,* Macmillan Pocket Tagore Edition. Macmillan India Limited. 1989, XII p. 8.

The romantic quest for the Innermost One is never a failure altogether. Since the poet is an ardent lover of the All Beautiful, he is never abandoned nor does he ever feel the absence of the cherished blessings of His gift. Here is an extraordinary mystic interpretation enriched in poignance of vision :

> *Palash* is the emblem of joy of the spring of life.
> Today to one bereft of honour
> In his poor hours you met
> Where I, the companionless, am alone
> Out of the courtyard of ceremonies
> On the sandy shores of the desert *sans* corn,
> Where from the vibrant garden of life of this earth
> My unwelcome days in unending current
> Like torn shoots are gone afloating
> At the end of the spring.
> Even then your gift is beyond miserliness
> The full price of youth you have offered in my heart *sans* lustre
> The ignorance of providence you denied not
> Her tiredness you did ameliorate,
> Conveyed in me and so am I all the time
> Prized with the welcome of Beauty, the invitation of the young.

— Rabindranath Tagore : *Arogya (Convalescence), Rabindra-Rachanavali,* Government of West Bengal, Calcutta, 1983, Vol. III No. 11, p. 828-829.

[Translated by Author.]

How does the poet, being welcomed in the world of Beauty Eternal, explain the strategy of the quest for the Innermost One in course of evaluation of his creative contributions ? What is the secret of inherent discipline and self-synchronization ? Let us listen to the words of the poet :

> My mind recollects words here and there
> As if the autumnal clouds are roaming after rains in the air
> Falsely does it travel without the string of work in the space
> Sometimes it paints in silver, reveals sometimes the golden colour in grace
> In the corner of the horizon does it build an image strange.
> Again and again it makes in a vacant mind of lines a change.
> That artistry of vapour is as if in the neglect of joy
> Nowhere is it responsible and so it makes its meaningless game of toy.
> Conscious is it to awake and so to be up and doing in work
> Slumber has nothing to do and so in distorted dreams to embark.
> The mood of the mind's dream is under the yoke of work
> No holiday does it enjoy in autonomy's park.
> With imaginations that crowd in its being free
> Like a flying bird does it build a nest in dream's artistry.
> And so feel I the evidence within me
> The oldest component of the universe is the dream's insanity.
> The process of creation checks it and perennial does it make
> With terrible strength does its authority intake.
> The skill of art is to arrest this boisterous fly
> For the unattainable to have a try.

— Rabindranath Tagore : *Arogya (Convalescence), Rabindra-Rachanavali,* Government of West

Bengal, Calcutta, 1983, Vol. III, No. 26, p. 836-837.

[Translated by Author.]

Is the endeavour for the unattainable a continual failure ? Is the quest for the Innermost One consequential to baffled breath of creative spree ? Tagore upholds a bright optimistic picture of the Most Endearing One rapt in sewing the woollen garments of Eternity :

When I fail to see you I think in sordid imagination
The Earth is conspiring aside under feet
To bid adieu,
The void sky do I want to clasp
Raising my two arms.
The dream tremblingly shatters
Behold I in drooping head you are weaving woollens
Sitting beside me.
The surest bliss of creation do I support.

— Rabindranath Tagore : *Rogashajyay, Rabindra - Rachanavali,* Government of West Bengal, Calcutta, 1983, Vol. III, No. 39, p. 811-812.

[Translated by Author.]

When will mankind be prepared to encounter the Innermost One exquisitely weaving with incomparable artistry ?

EDUCATION FOR CREATIVITY AND TALENT : TAGOREAN PERSPECTIVES

Creativity, always an inner efflorescence, is what man as man should be as the most rational animal. It *is* or ought to be his real identity-*c'est moi.* Each 'I' is the womb of 'we' pregnant with the essence or excellence of man. Education comes forward to caress each 'I' to christen it by means of culture of creativity and talent to present the one great Family of Man with recrystallized 'We'-s.

An eternal apostle of creativity and talent, Rabindranath Tagore urges education to be true to life. He himself has the bitterness of education *sans* creativity and exercise of individual talent—a truant haplessly seeking the real *alma mater* in not less than four so-called educational institutions of creative imprisonment— *'dasta panchtar andaman'*, as he has most significantly remarked. As an ardent exponent of emancipation of creative spontaneity by means of education—living, pulsating, nurturing every talent with care and caution, and, of course, psychological—he advocates for the education of sympathy to cast aside the age-long ills of apathy and ignorance which are, as he gravely remarks, 'the worst forms of bondage' for mankind. However, to explore and explain creativity in terms of education, he emphasizes on the education through Nature and the education for joy—*ananda*—

that enrich individual talent. Psychologically, when Tagore is concerned with education, he is actually concerned with the evolution of consciousness—some inner value for which the learner endlessly strives.

The wails of the creative learner lost in the moratorium of mechanical drudgeries in the walled buildings of educational institutions deeply touched Tagore. He categorically calls out for dismantling the caged atmosphere of learning *'harinbarir prachir'* as he has aptly described and emphasized on pupil-creativity in order to be justified to individual talent and fulness of life. In this connection, one might recall the following invaluable words :

> That to create our own world has been the purpose of God, we see when we find that, even as children we had our one and only pleasure in that play where, with trifling materials, we gave expression to our imagination. That is more valuable to us as children than gold or banknotes or anything else. The same thing is true with regard to every human individual. We forget this value of the individual creative power because our minds become obsessed with the artificial value which is made prevalent in society by other people's valuation of a particular manner of living, a particular style of respectability. We force ourselves to accept that imposition and we kill the most precious gift that God has given us, the gift of creation which comes from His own Nature.[1]

Objectives

The Tagorean objectives of education for efflorescence of creativity and talent may be spelt out as follows :

(i) to encourage every learner to exercise his critical thinking and creative appreciation in a joyous atmosphere.

(ii) to stimulate each learner to come in close contact with Nature, revitalize his endeavour of creativity and talent and formulate his own unparalleled views and opinions bearing a significant stamp of creative consciousness.

(iii) to enable each learner to identify and discover the inherent creative urge in association with the living and pulsating experiences he receives from Nature.

(iv) to ensure each learner to be so justified to his creative talent as to synchronize aesthetic and spiritual education and discover newer avenues of creative and critical excellence.

(v) to encourage each learner to channelize his creative abilities towards exploration and dissemination of the fulness in man.

(vi) to enable each learner to find out better avenues of introspection by means of education for creative excellence.

(vii) to provide for each learner ample opportunities to be christened in aesthetic sensibilities for efflorescence of creative uniqueness.

(viii) to allow pupils to discover the inner essence of spiritualism that broadens the domain of creative vision.

(ix) to inspire each learner to explore out of his creative ingenuities newer avenues of religion as an inseparable part of mankind.

(x) to stimulate pupils to explore freedom from diverse dimensions of creativity and talent.

Creativity, always an infinite delight as Tagore strongly emphasizes in his thoughts and experiments on education, finds best sustenance from Nature. Like Wordsworth he believes that Nature teaches more 'of moral evil and of good' than moralists or spiritual thinkers, but unlike Wordsworth be delves deep into the manifold avenues of delight by which Nature enriches the creative mind with the perfumes of promise. Indeed, Tagore visualizes and actualizes, too, in his experiments on education, the fact that creativity has its affinity with Nature that brings forth in abundance a joyous atmosphere for intrinsic awakening. What is greatly needed in education is to create a joyous atmosphere of learning in association with Nature so that the development of inner creative sensibilities becomes a reality not by reading books alone but by continually reading oneself creatively and critically and writing in a language of originality, poignance and beauty. As Tagore warns.

> Let no such superstition be nurtured in the mind of children that learning is reading books. It is to be known at every step that the treasures of books are accumulated from the storehouse of Nature, and this should be, and we also have the authority to have it in the same way. As the disturbances of books are taking place to a great extent, I would like to assert it more emphatically.[2]

Strategies

What are the strategies that Tagore triggers for education for emancipation of creativity and talent ? A study of his own educational thoughts and experiments on education provides us with the following parameters :

(a) an introspective study of the mind of man from diverse points of view—social, moral, intellectual, aesthetic and spiritual.

(b) a creative exercise of erudition and individual talent in terms of real-life situation that embraces work-experience under favourable and trying situation.

(c) a certain sense of awareness for physical growth and development in close association with Nature that "brings from her depth responses in colours and perfume, music and movement, her incessant self-revelation, continual wonders of the unexpected"[3].

(d) an endless study of the vast sky, sunrise and sunset, stars and the moon etc. that bring forth wonder in the process of creative endeavour.

(e) an indepth study of the self in poignance of promise and askance to be in unison with the supreme self—the All Beautiful—that highlights the zenith of creativity through creative illumination.

(f) an unwarranted and spontaneous exercise of freedom of thought and expression by means of participation in innovative and living performing arts side by side with aesthetic exercise of simplicity, modesty and purity of creative excellence.

The education of science, the education that fillips the spirit of enquiry is, as Tagore advocates, the education for efflorescence of creative talent. It is interesting to note how he himself creates an ideal atmosphere of learning science in his own school at Santiniketan where each pupil is allowed to study the flora and the fauna in and around Santiniketan. The teacher is there with them, always active and agile, dynamic and creative himself whose only assignment is to enkindle the inherent spirit of creative consciousness in every learner. Furthermore, he allows the avenues of scientific enquiry wide open to have the inner essence of science which, according to him, is not only creative but also spiritual in essence :

> ***truth is spiritual in itself and truly materialistic is the mind of the animal which is unscientific and, therefore, unable to cross the dark screen of appearance, of accidents, and reach the deeper region of universal laws.[4]

It is interesting to note how Tagore himself was devoted to the dissemination of creative and critical enquiry by means of writing and editing books on science and inviting scientists and scholars of repute to write easy to learn books for children and juvenile readers in general and adult learners in particular. His own unusual and extra-ordinary venture to boost creativity by means of writing a book on science in Bengali at the age of seventy-six entitled *Visva-Parichay* shows how keen he is to unfold the windows of creative talent and scientific approach to life. This writing a book on science is not at all out of his sudden manifestation of scientific temperament. Right from his boyhood, as he admits, he is brought up in an ideal atmosphere of scientific knowledge and enquiry which has all along protected him from being conservative and sentimental in attitude. He is also indebted to his pursuit of science because this has strengthened him enough to orient himself through intellectual discipline even when he is essentially a poet and there is a great deal of vulnerability of being swept away by the overflowing sentimental current of imagination. To expand the arena of consciousness and to be justified to one's creative talent, education geared to science is, as he himself translates into reality in his educational experimentations at Santiniketan not only necessary for sustenance of creativity but also for elevation of human life and human dignity. This is why in his preface to the book on science entitled *Visva-Parichay* he emphasizes on introducing science at the very beginning of education for one child who might develop and exercise its individual and unique creative and critical askance and approach to learning. He also refers that this endeavour to widen the children's outlook on science as a creative and pragmatic endeavour might not fulfil its highest zenith of excellence just at the outset from all possible avenues, but, then, this will definitely be a bold endeavour to do away with age-old blind faiths, ignorance and superstitions with which the conservative mind is infected. Let all learners be invited to the courtyard of science, if not in full intensity to its deeper levels of creativity and critical poignance.

Rabindranath also makes an altogether newer avenue of efflorescence of spiritualism by means of making a unison between the traditional Eastern spiritual outlook and the Western scientific approach. The blessings of Western science and technology would, as he rightly asserts, find best exposure in spiritual endeavour only when creativity is evenly balanced with individual area of excellence. Such a move cannot but yield worthy dividends in the onward march of mankind.

Keeping in view all the time that education for true social change is the education of science for emancipation of all round development of creative humanity, Tagore makes a valiant endeavour to disseminate the education of science on a war footing through the mother tongue. While on the one hand, he continually goes on contributing scientific and technological articles in prominent journals like the *Bharati* and the *Bhander* in Bengali, on the other, he encourages teachers in his own school at Santiniketan, like Jagadananda Roy and others, to write books on science in simple and lucid language for children to crystallize their creative talent.

To arrest topsy turvy in education right from the beginning so that the learner at his very young age is gifted with wide avenues of advancement and freedom of independent thinking and creativity, Tagore emphasizes on education that fosters thinking and creative learners. And, for this, he urges on education through the mother tongue which alone ensures a sound foundation of learning. His own exposition in this connection is worth revealing :

> The power of thought and the power of imagination are indispensable to us for discharging the duties of life. We cannot do without those two powers if we want to live like real men. And unless we cultivate them in childhood we cannot have them when we are grown up.
>
> Our present system of education, however, does not allow us to cultivate them. We have to spend

> many years of our childhood in learning a foreign language taught by men not qualified for the job. To learn the English language is difficult enough, but to familiarize ourselves with English thought and feeling is even more difficult, and takes a long time during which our thinking capacity remains inactive for lack of an outlet.
>
> To read without thinking is like accumulating building materials without building anything. After we have accumulated a mountainous pile of mortar, lime and sand, and of bricks, beams and rafters, we suddenly get an order from the University to do the roof of a three-storeyed house. So we instantly climb to the top of our pile and beat it down incessantly for two years, until it becomes level and somewhat resembles the flat roof of a house. But could this pile be called a house ? Has it window to let in air and light ? Could a man make it his home for the whole of his life ? Has it order, beauty, harmony ?
>
> There is no doubt that a great deal of material is now collected in our country for building the edifice of the mind, much greater than at any other time in its history. But we must not make the mistake of thinking that by learning to collect we have learnt to build. Good results follow only when accumulation and building are carried on, step by step, at the same time.[5]

For efflorescence of the creative talent, Tagore makes a radical approach to aesthetics in order to make a real and living synchronization between intellectual exercise and emotional and aesthetic serenity. Moreover, he elevates the finer sensibilities of the learner by allowing him to enter and appreciate fine arts, music, poetry etc. that abundantly contribute to the manifestation of creative potentiality. As he poignantly observes:

> Our conscious mind occupies only a superficial layer of our life; the sub-conscious mind is almost fathomless in its depth. There the wisdom of countless ages grows up beyond our view. Our sub-conscious, where dwells our soul, must also have its adequate media of expression. These media are poetry and music and the arts; here the complete personality of man finds its expression.[6]

The marriage between Truth and Creativity as Tagore visualizes is possible only when a learner makes an earnest adventure in the domain of the beyonding of consciousness. This is possible only when the learner is baptized within by the serene 'I' that makes unending unison with Truth. Let the mind strive towards inner perfection just as the bud awaits emancipation in flowering. Let all avenues of curiosity and askance be backed by a living, pulsating approach to joyousness and spontaneity in the domain of advancement of learning. What is the best outcome of learning ? How far is creativity desirable in education and life ? Here is Tagore's categorical answer :

> The knowledge that is merely an informatics, bears very little worth, for that diminishes within a limited area of knowing. But the knowledge that is not an informatics but a theory, that is, which cannot be completed within a single incident, which is prevalent both in innumerable incidents of the past and which would manifest itself even in innumerable incidents of the future, which is not only expressed in a particular incident but is also existent as an unexpressed one in the endless—in that knowledge our joy prevails.[7]
>
> [Translated by Author.]

For the Spotless and Serene

Creativity, an unending wonder, awaits a *metanoia*—a transvaluation of values in terms of education for being. Lost is the mind that has already become a routinized nonsense—a 69-E as Tagore portrays in *The Red Oleanders.* Lost also is the human creative impulse that rediscovers the religion of man by means of the education of sympathy and love—the education of excellence. The sky of the mind—the *cidakas*—awaits harbouring of human consciousness in the dynamic approach to education for creative perfection. Automations, mechanomania writ large in a battered and bruised global society are to be reshuffled with the creative adventure for the prized perfection of individual talent. A newer beginning for such a creative ecstasy cannot but endear Tagorean thoughts and experiments on education for creativity and talent.

Meanwhile, why not join the prayer to inhale the creative perfume of promise in serenity ?

> The same stream of life that runs through my veins night and day runs through the world and dances in rhythmic measures.
>
> It is the same life that shoots in joy through the dust of the earth in numberless blades of grass and breaks into tumultuous waves of leaves and flowers.
>
> It is the same life that is rocked in the ocean-cradle of birth and of death in ebb and in flow.
>
> I feel my limbs are made glorious by the touch of this world of life. And my pride is from the life-throb of ages dancing in my blood this moment.[8]

REFERENCES

1. Rabindranath Tagore : "The School Master", *The Modern Review,* Calcutta, October 1924, p. 373.

2. Rabindranath Tagore : *'Avaran', Siksha,* Visva-Bharati, 1973, p. 75. (Translated by Author)

3. Rabindranath Tagore : "A Poet's School", *The Visva-Bharati Quarterly,* Santiniketan, October 1926, p. 212.

4. *Visva-Bharati Bulletin* : "Rabindranath Tagore's visit to Canada and Japan", Visva-Bharati, No. 14, p. 72.

5. Rabindranath Tagore : "The Vicissitudes of Education", *Towards Universal Man,* Asia Publishing House, Bombay, 1961. p. 43-44.

6. Rabindranath Tagore : "The Centre of Indian Culture", *Towards Universal Man,* Asia Publishing House, Bombay, 1961, p. 225.

7. Rabindranath Tagore : "Santiniketan", *Rabindra-Rachanavali,* Government of West Bengal, Calcutta, Tagore Birth Centenary Education. 1961, Vol. XII, p. 285.

8. Rabindranath Tagore : *Song Offerings,* Macmillan India Limited, Macmillan Pocket Tagore Edition, 1983, No. 69, p. 46-47.

THE LOVE SONGS OF RABINDRANATH TAGORE

The songs of Rabindranath Tagore bring forth an eternal sense of serenity and poignance. They inhale the spirit of spontaneity and freshness of vision. They expose the inherent sense of joy and sorrow, laughter and tears, pleasure and pain, happiness and languishment.

Perhaps the most thrilling and pulsating theme of Tagore's songs is love. Love lights the inner world of human feelings and sensibilities and draws man nearer to man. It enriches man to be worthy of his serene vision of unison with the All Beautiful. It comes alone or in silence but opens up a flood of light enkindling the vision of the man of the heart—*maner manush.* Again, it unfolds all inner constraints in the tunings of humble submission that ennobles it with the perfume of promise.

Admittedly, Tagore intensifies love in loneliness not because it has its softer appeal to the mind but essentially because it comes like a fresh air to begin life anew. The sonorous music of the *veena* that beckons him introspectively is a serene signal for him to prepare himself to accord a joyous welcome to the beloved :

Whose *veena* played on in sonorous tunes
In my life new and serene
Like the morning lotus did my heart bloom
For the two decent feet I know not
All grace makes up, all sweetness
At every twinkling of eyes is the heart filled in joy
The gentle breeze brings forth new awakening
By dispelling the veil of the heart, I know not
What a pain aches in the breast in happiness and
sorrow
My words do fail to spell out
My aspirations today ring in the world
In pangs of pain the river and the woods tremble.[1]

Love turns into a humble submission to the beloved not because love is, as Tagore introspects, effeminate but because it is serene with divine poignance. The *veena* that tunes on awaits that moment of fulfilment in the eternal prayer of love :

Make me thy *veena,* hold me, O hold me up
The strings would tune on in lovely fingers
With thy hands tender like the lotus, touch my
heart
My heart would murmur in muse in thy ears
Sometimes in happiness, in sorrow sometimes would
cry looking at thee
Silently would it lie at the feet in forgetfulness
None knows in what tuning anew would the muse
march towards the vacant
The message of joy would move towards the shore of
the endless.[2]

Love comes and bids good-bye serenely and silently. It leaves a note of separation painful and heavy with sorrow in darkness. It brings forth tears in the forms of clouds covering the morning sun. The union becomes more poignant with the unwelcome and unknown adornment of separation :

When didst thou adorn me with the garland of
welcome in dream,

the garland of pain ?
In the morning do I see in the clouded sun
the farewell flute plays on with poured out tears
Thou didst come and go in secret
And I didn't see you feasting my eyes.
Thou didst fasten me with the strings of sorrow in darkness
and adorn me with ornaments soaked with the pains of separation.[3]

Love leaves for the poet tears in adoration. The flute plays on, the flute of evanescent sweetness, the flute that promises union of the lover and the beloved beyond the distance unreachable. The beauty of sorrow makes him lost direction. Even then love remains alive in mind with the eternal presence of the beloved :

Thou hast made me weep with the stroke of thy love
In intense pain I feel joy in me
I shall go to the shores of the unreachable in search of thee.
Let pain tune on during my journey on every avenue
The flute plays on in the heart, streams roll on thro' eyes
The beauty of sorrow made me lose direction
Thou wouldst snatch away all, yet wouldst thou leave nothing
The mind does not desire to depart, O in what a mess hast thou bound me ![4]

Where does the poet seek emancipation ? It is in love and love alone. The greatest meditation of love awaits a flight like a bird in the heart of the beloved. The tired days run like streams only to terminate in the bliss of the dense-deep night of the beloved. Passion runs high in intoxication but then the signal of success anew seeks adoration within the beloved. Here is the benign revelation :

I know in thy love the message of all love mingles
I seek my salvation in it alone at the day's end
The greatest meditation of love is there, all its bonds are loosened
In thy heart is the sky of the bird of my heart
O Dear, know I that all the streams of my tired days
Become tireless in the bliss of thy dense-deep night
The touch of the earth in my body has become lively with thy drink
The very wealth of my dust adores within Thee in a new pattern.[5]

That the sky of the bird in the poet's heart as a lover is really in the heart of the beloved living far away on the shores of the sea makes love more intense and soul-stirring. The ears of the lover, too, are in agonising expectations of listening to the song of the beloved, leaving aside the barriers of language or distance. The words of appreciation to the song of love are perhaps the sweetest compliments from a poet's heart:

Know I, O foreigner, I know you
On the shores of the sea is your abode
In the autumn morning and at the *madhavi* night have I seen you
In the core of my heart, O foreigner, have I seen you.
Placing my ears in the sky have I listened to your song
I've submitted my life to you, O foreigner.
After trekking the world, to a new land have I come at last,
A guest am I at your doorstep, O foreigner.[6]

The same adoration is expressed through the words of gratitude that the poet conveys in listening to the tune of the *veena* unknown which aches his heart. He wants to come out of his room only due to the wild intoxication of the loving tune in loneliness :

No more can I forbear
O the tune aches in the mind I fail to express in words
Down bends the creeper-like heart with the burden of painful flowers,
No more can I bear that
In my serene heart today
O, what a wind trembled in joyous and restless murmurs
On this stoic morning who is that expert that has attuned the *veena* unknown
No more can I remain in the room.[7]

The language that the poet wants to convey to the beloved cannot be the language of music. And so he tunes on the flute amidst the star-studded night. But, it is a bizarre one as it ebbs away with that of the beloved. Therefore, he gives back the tune in floating darkness—the tune that amazes with a beloved's yearning for love :

No words have I
Know I only to look spreading the silent heart
Darkest night am I *sans* light
spreading countless stars
In vain hope do I await endless path
When you play on the flute tunes afloat
In the depth of silence in the perplexed wind
Crossing o'er the sea of slumber
The echo of your own tune do I give you back
Who knows if it reaches the shores of your dream
Floating o'er darkness unending.[8]

The poet does not want to depart from the door of the beloved even when the gloom of separation overcasts him. Separation to him is like a sea unfathomable and vast, and so he cannot but lose himself in the avenue of the unknown. It deeply aches him to think that he has failed to compliment the love of the beloved in return. A sense of utter sorrow engulfs the entire canvas of his mind. The broken world of timelessness brings forth for him moments of restlessness that echo and vibrate in poignance of love in agonising separation :

My mind desires not to depart
Crossing thy door I lose myself
Immersed, as it were, in the unfathomable sea of separation
Trekking on the way, everything do I behold to be false
Timeless does the wide world beckon behind
All the time does my mind ache
Ah, nothing did I offer thee
When I depart I halt at every step
And return for reasons unknown.[9]

How does the Poet endear the beloved ? How does he unfold the inner vision of love now lost and regained immediately afterwards with distance and nearness ? Let the union of eyes and exchange of sweet words between the lover and the beloved arrest the agonies of the night and the wailings of the heart :

None feels the mind of the other
each comes nearer and departs
Why does the smile of endearment
die down in tears
When the wind wept away,
flowers bloomed not with hearts wide open
Why do they lonely wither away in the hours of evening ?
Look at the face, unite eyes with eyes
Cover not the sweet words of the heart in your heart
The night will bid farewell, no more will we speak
The morning will mourn with the wailings of the heart.[10]

To look at the face and unite eyes with eyes and thus to unfold the beauty of life have the same efflorescence of love in Nature where the rose is personified to bloom and speak like the beloved. The dewdrops, the southern wind, the well-disciplined flower-maids await the blooming of the poet's friend, the Rose. The evening stars, too, are eager to behold the countenance of the flower of flowers. Countless bees and tender green leaves are also on the tiptoe of expectation. When would the Rose love along with the nectar like moon's smile ? A keen sense of passionate love symbolized through the Rose and crystallized in the warmth of simplicity accelerates in a sonorous atmosphere of picturesque imageries so ardently drawn by the poet :

> Tell, Rose, tell me
> When you will bloom, my friend
> Everywhere the flowers bloom the moon shines with her nectar smile
> Softly does the wind breathe, sweetly are the birds singing
> When will you bloom, my friend ?
> Dew-drops have fallen in the morn, the southern wind is blowing in the evening
> Flower-maids are in rows nearby
> Yonder are the evening stars at the backdrop of leaves
> Eager to behold thy countenance
> From a distance has the wind turned up
> Countless bees are moving close
> Tender green leaves are with peeping eyes
> And they all ask together :
> When will you bloom, O friend ?[11]

The flute of love has a penetrating effect in the love-lorn soul. It is the flute that makes love more poignant and soul-stirring than anything. Even death is smiled away with the union of the lover and the beloved by means of the flute. As the muse spells out,

> They endear others as their own and make themselves alien,

With the sound of the flute outside, they leave the
room,
With weal and woe do they love.
With smiling face do they forbear pain
And make death eternally dependent on life.[12]

The Yamuna might be a holy place for reunion between the lover and the beloved. As love triumphs over colour or complexion, it is now better to submit to the lover even with his lone smile through the corners of his eyes or his appearance only in dreams. The pulsating heart of the beloved eagerly awaiting the lover is facing the two alternatives. The muse of love becomes vibrant in dramatic poignance :

Not yet have I seen him with eyes, only the flute
have I heard to play on
The mind or life whatsoever, have I already
surrendered
His mien is black as I've heard, it's better not to see
him.
Friend, tell me if to the Yamuna shall I go to fetch
water.
Only in dream did he come, in the corners of eyes
did he laugh
From that time, friend, I remain in awe—I am lost
in thought to open my eyes
Whoever desires does tread on the way to the
flower garden
Whoever desires does look at the feet of the
Kadam tree
Friend, tell me if I with eyes raised shall look at
any one
Friend, shall I look at any one with eyes raised ?[13]

The spring of love is the spring of the moment of happiness. It is the spring of union after a long time—a union of the mind and the heart to speak out in fullness of love. The desires are young and the heart throbs for the moment of union. The heart awaits the lover to adorn the seat and the Poet poignantly muses on :

> Is the spring come for the first time in life today ?
> With young desire, ah, how the heart throbs !
> The young in life becomes living
> In the world brimmed with happiness, the mind wants to expand
> Whom does it want to be seated in the heart ?
> All through shall I wander for her.[14]

The moment of union is the moment of love. It is the moment of happiness and joy. For this moment of moments the Poet desires no more than the lovely smile and countenance of the beloved, the soft nimble movements of her lips and the passionate words of love. Just so much and not anything more. And with these, the love that the poet so ardently feels for her would guide him in his lone endless journey from time immemorial. Here is the frank confession :

> After many a day did I come today to visit you
> Fear not, in happiness remain, not much shall I stay
> For a moment have I come
> Only the countenance shall I see, and listen to the words if you utter
> Or shall I traverse from land to land by looking at your smile aside.[15]

Is the beloved a dream ? Is she beyond visibility ? Why does she move away from flower to flower like a butterfly ? Should she not adorn the poet's love ? Does she want to remain far away from the lover ? Now when she has come for once, why not stand for a while ? Let love be brightened with the halo of exchange of vision between the lover and the beloved in serene purity—a treasure eternal :

> Return not, go not back
> Stand, stand for a while on the seat of the heart
> Like restless wind

Why do you tread on from flower to flower
from one garden to the other
I want to catch hold of you but I fail
As if with dream you are framed
Come, O come, let me see you once with full eyes
With care do I treasure you up
Amid life shall I wrap you up
With flowers shall I entwine you
All thro' the day and the night
You will be in unison with the tender bed of love.[16]

How does the beloved actually pine for love ? What happens when the whole atmosphere beckons her to be alive in the spirit of love ? The web of love is already woven with the tune of music brought forth with the humming of bees. The words of the lover have already been conveyed in the unknown language of music. When would the lover come to bring an end to the agonising counting of days and hours and moments ? The askance of the beloved is the askance of love mesmerized in *maya* :

The bee came in the room humming
Whose words does he convey to me ?
In the light did he come with the message of the
flower-awakening news of the sky
Where *madhabi* blooms in the forest
All day long does he go on disseminating that news
How can I remain in the room, ah,
how the mind aches
How the day wanes counting on days
What a *maya* does he brush on
and makes me forget all my work
The day passes on weaving webs in tunes of music
Whose words does he convey to me ?[17]

The aching of love is the aching of the inner soul that awaits emancipation in union. For the poet, love entwines the two souls pining for union eternal. The trap of love is spread all over the world. It is the true lover or the true beloved who identifies love for union and emancipation of the soul. The flute that tunes on, declares the release of pride that entraps the mind. And so the adoration of pain that love brings forth is the adoration of simplicity that is expressed in tears of love. It is an adoration wilful and, therefore, challenging to submit to love with the tuning of the flute :

> The trap of love is lain all thro' the world
> Who knows where one is trapped
> All the glory, alas, tears apart
> Eyes flow in tears
> Only do you want to have in this happy earth
> Know ye not how to give yourself
> With the shadow of happiness will you leave unnoticed
> Pain will you wilfully adore
> When the flute plays on you know not
> Pride plies away
> In strings does life scramble.[18]

How does the beloved want to illuminate the hours of efflorescence ? How does she look forward to the hallowed moments of union ? What is her inner strategy for participating in the festival of love ? Here is her earnest appeal to friends :

> Time seems to sail on
> Come, ye come to the flower garden.
> Flower came out ablooming in light,
> In shadow do they wither away
> I wish I would adorn him
> With the garland as my mind wishes
> Where is that garland to be sewn ah, where he came
> The waves of the Yamuna roll on, time sails on.[19]

Waiting for the beloved is waiting for moments of union and illumination. Love holds the key to this union of the mind and the heart. Distance only draws each other nearer and nearer. The dense forest of separation is the canvas of oblivion.

It is also the canvas of reminiscence. Even darkness has light within. And so, the darkness of separation has within it the light of union awaiting liberation of efflorescence in the festival of love. Dreams are but prior preparations of an aching heart to encounter the never lost embodiment of love. Who beckons that ever existent love, and how ? It is the lover and the lover alone who knows that his flute will eternally play on the tune of living reminiscence of love. As the poet unfolds the wonder of love :

In what a dense forest did I lose her
In what a backdrop of reminiscence and oblivion of
longlost life
In light and darkness today
Sometimes do I behold her, sometimes not—
What a sea of dreams with the happiness of unison
did she come across
Betwixt the existent and the non-existent
My flute plays on with the *ragini* of *chhayanat*
The dancing of shadow at the *vakul* tree is in
unison with the fragrance of flowers.
I know not what makes the mind mad
Which danseus' whirling dress-end touches my
body.[20]

With dreams and songs in a repeated fashion love mingles in the sands of time. The throbbing heart waits for the grand encounter. But when would she appear ? Song after song hail the moment, the tune goes on uninterrupted but even then, the aching love persists in the never ending hours of love :

Day after day passes, beside the way I sit
Song after song do I sing in the wind of the spring
The hours do not want to wane and so is the game
by attuning—
The mirage of ragini is in the flickerings of dreams.
Day after day passes, no encounter with you takes
place
Song after song do I sing, alone do I remain seated.

Lest the tune comes to a halt, you do not come nearer
Love aches one whom one loves.[21]

Indeed, in love there is a promise for reunion. With the waning of time and with all distance between the lover and the beloved, the bonds of love and union become more intense and serene. Here is the muse of the traveller of love at the doorsteps of the beloved leaving the message of his arrival and that of his farewell to step ahead towards the shore of the endless :

At her doors did I come, in darkness did I call on
Holding on the bar, I gave a jolt.
Hours passed on, no response did I receive
Ah, I failed to see her.
But ere I depart from here, this letter did I leave behind.

No matter if I meet you or not,
Know, O dear, that I came to see you.
Towards the shore of the endless do I go back.[22]

That the banquet of union between the lover and the beloved is a promonition to languishment is a new experience derived from the withering and drooping down of flowers. The garland of joy turns into a garland of sorrow and forgetting. The sudden encounter between the lover and the beloved after long-lost days is the moment of the game of tears. Forgettings serve as the backdrop of such an encounter, and the moments become alive with the resonance of serene love. Here is a frank confession by the Poet :

When the banquet of union came to an end
I thought I won't forget shedding tears any more
Day by day in the dust of the path
Flowers droop down from the garland.
I knew not when the hours of forgettings did come
Day by day the labyrinth of the breast
Became hard unnoticed
I thought my tears would no longer roll on

A sudden encounter on the way, unending weepings
In the backdrop of forgettings did the game of tears
go on.[23]

Every moment of union of languished love is a moment of lovely hesitation. A dramatic sensation pervades the mind pulsating and thrilling with the resonance of love. The very canvas of the living moments of love—the full brimmed evening, the smile in the corners of eyes, the trembling heart in the lonely doorsteps, the flight of the young stork, the agonising heart—leave behind the askance unending : Is love mingled in the pain of fragrance in the drenched jasmine ? The drama of human love is perhaps a painful history of never lost feelings and sordid images with which the hearts of the lover and the beloved are intertwined. As the poet muses to adroitly prepare the dramatic setting :

What a hesitation did you leave in the mind on that day
in the full-brimmed evening
On your departure from the door your turned away your
thoughtful endurance
What a word was there in your mind,
What a smile did you leave behind in the corner of your
eyes !
With a trembling heart I think a-sitting,
In the distant world you remain.
A young stork is flying in the sky
The pains within me are her companion
For once do I desire to ask you what you did not say at the
time of farewell
Did it remain, O dear, in the pain adorned in fragrance of
the drenched jasmine ![24]

The song of love that the poet sings becomes an introspective reactionary. It stealthily penetrates into his mind and overpowers quite majestically. The kindred atmosphere all around becomes a happy partner to such a song of love. Even the touch of the restless wind on the forehead makes the poet very sensitive and passionate. He beckons the traveller of the vanishing path to accompany him in the spring tide :

> The song of mine own steals my mind behind my sight
> And takes me afloating beyond all endings.
> Yonder on the shores the early spring is in glamour with flowers.
> Turbulent wind blows from there and touches my sail
>
> Where do you, my unknown companion,
> Spend the night of languishment in loneliness ?
> Come, come, O traveller of the vanishing path.
> Dangling is my boat in spring tide.[25]

The lotusland of life efflorescent and vibrant in love nursles reminiscence of union between the lover and the beloved. Let the cup of farewell be full of the juice of happy union. Let every parting moment be glorified with the new promise of reunion. The tears of sorrow are the pearls of happiness and that happiness makes love meaningful and significant. The muse of love becomes the eternal muse of human destiny. As the poet sings :

> Let the cup of union be filled in with the wine of reminiscence
> Give me that back by bringing on the festival of union
> In tears of agony in the core of silence
> Let the new message of the heart be in secret effulgence.
> Alone you are on the way to be trekked
> Darkness will prevail in eyes, the line of light in meditation.
> All the day the pleasant wine will you pour in the mind
> In the lotusland of life, the goddess of languishment does adore.[26]

When the playtime of love is over, spring too bids goodbye. And what remains ? The light of the morning simply weeps, the thread of union shatters. Everything turns out to be false. The vacant eyes wait for regaining the happy moments of love. Now is the time to pick up the left-out flowers of love. Now is the time for total languishment beyond thought beyond dream :

Thou hast made my morning light weep
Tearing off the string of the garland of union
Whate'er is left behind has all become meaningless
With eyes feasting towards the far away do I remain seated.
One by one do I go on
Picking up the withered flowers from the farewell path
Never thought I that no trace of that day would last
In what game did I spend the hours of the early spring ![27]

The appreciation of love by the beloved springs from the sea of gratitude. It is a gratitude that is lost in the web of enchantment. The words find no language. The feelings are mesmerized, the emotions stifled and silent in the canvas of darkness amidst countless stars. Sleep bids farewell in utter astonishment. The tune of the flute comes to the heart only to go back trekking along darkness to the shores of the dream for the lover. The tune of the flute is the tune of lover that knows no defeat. But, then, where is love *sans* adoration ? Here is the frank confession of the beloved :

No words have I
Know I only to look spreading the silent heart
Darkest night am I *sans* light
spreading countless stars
In vain hope do I await endless path
When you play on the flute, tunes afloat
In the depth of silence in the perplexed wind
Crossing o'er the sea of slumber

The echo of your own tune do I give you back
Who knows if it reaches the shore of your dream
Floating o'er darkness unending.[28]

To wait for the lover is to wait for fulfilment of love. But is love fulfilled ? Is the vision of love complete in what the lover and the beloved ardently desire ? Why, then, is waiting directed towards the tune of the flute ? Why is adornment of silence in pain ? Perhaps love wants so. Perhaps from the depth of sorrow of languishment love takes a new image of perfection. Love is like a *vakul* flower waiting for unison that does not even care for identification. As the muse spells out :

My life have I entwined with thee in the spring of tunes
Know ye not, in meditation unknown do I have thee.
The perfume of *vakul* is in unison with that meditation.
The rhymes of the poet synchronize with that meditation
Know ye not, I've covered thy name with the coverings of colourful shade
Thy beautiful image
Do I place in the light of the early spring
In the pleasing spring do I play on the flute in the distant horizon
With golden light does thy dress-end tremble
with the intoxication of the rhyme of the song.[29]

Love in languishment is love in fulfilment. It is love that urges the mind and the heart to find out the poignant *ragini* for happiness and contentment. It is love that beckons the full moon to spread its splendour in the form of the aura of love. The whole world is agog with the vibrant feeling of love immortalized. The night of love is the night of eternal sweetness. As for the poet, languishment gets a new language in pleasant surprise :

Languishment has become pleasant in the sweet tonight
A profound *ragini* tunes out in pain

Filling in with the night of the full moon
What a plaintive mirage does the restless thirst for absence of meeting bring forth !
In the petals of eyes
With air adorned with nice streams of fragrance from the distant,
The lost wayfarer becomes weary in my heart.
Whose message murmurs in the nets of leaves in tunes and rhythm unknown.
And with it rings along my bunches of bangles.[30]

Love disseminated in notes of the plaintive flute is love reminiscent in sweet and touching images. It is love that is always picturesque and vibrant with the language of silence. The pains of love unknown find an altogether new language of exposition. The restless wind on the shores of the sea, the lovelorn shadow under the forest trees, the hummings of sweet exchange of words between the lover and the beloved—all create a living atmosphere of love beyond time and space. Distance matters very little. Love wipes out whatever distance acts as a barrier to reminiscence. It acts like a reflector of sweet memories and pleasant moments. What a pleasure it is to muse on the days and moments of love from abroad !

Who goes playing on the plaintive flute in a foreign boat
That very tune touched me.
Plying on that tune whose pain unknown of the languished heart from a long distance comes afloating
In the restless wind
Under the shadow of the forest
That very resonance touched me.
Hearing that today amidst the heart in the lonely life abroad
The drenched *bhairavi* silently tunes on in the early autumn dew
The picture flashes on in the light and in music—
Who treads on along the lonely riverpath

With idle steps to fill in the picher with water
Beneath the shadow of the forest.[31]

Is love dejected a forewarning or a warning for love awaiting fulfilment ? Why, then, are the eyes automatically welled up in tears ? Why is the mind so restless and perturbed ? Silence adds a new definition to such a painful and agonised love. The very thought of love uncared for makes love more purified and resonant :

Why the eye itself is flooded in water
Why the mind so quivers
As if all of a sudden what a word is recalled.
No recalling O dear, and yet I recall
All around everything is pleasantly silent
Why the life of mine pines in crying
Why, why-the mind so quivers
As if whose words have pained me
As if someone has gone back uncared
That very absence of care does ring in the heart
As if all of a sudden what a word is recalled
No recalling O dear, and yet I recall.[32]

With the flow of tears, the pain of love gets a new definition, a new meaning. It evolves a new sense of love that shines out in brilliance of silence.

Ah with pain do my words sink, sink down
in the flow of tears did I lose the tune
Your boat is on the water of the sea
On the shores do I roam about

Ah, no room for me on your golden boat—
Where do I find the way in darkness ?

Ah, in desparation do my eyes pine away
Towards the door do I stand and go on seeing

None tells me about the room where that lamp burns
Alone do I remain seated on the way
On the sea-shore of the eternal night.[33]

To remain alone is to ponder over the poignance of love. Love in loneliness finds the best language with the bliss of silence. The agonies of encounter with the moments of love become thrilling. The anxieties of the heart run like a whistling train. The long waiting for the beloved has a new and altogether dramatic significance. The picture is vivid and at the same time ardent with the resonance of love. The lover with the garland of the flowers of smile, the fruit of sorrow as revealed in the train of tears, the sudden outburst of the maiden for union, the long awaited and greatly expected victory of love—all make a colourful and vibrant ceremony of love in the canvas of serene moments :

> On her hands was the garland of the flowers of
> smile adorned with countless colour
> With me was the burden of the fruit of sorrow
> filled in with the juice of tears
> All of a sudden that beautiful maiden came and said
> 'Do please come, let's exchange ?
> I looked at her face. What a beauty !
> She is unkind but lovely
> My offerings of full-flooded rains did she accept,
> curiously she looked
> Taking her garland of the new early spring
> I clasped it on the breast
> Victory to me' said she with a smile while going
> Hurriedly did she depart
> In the evening did I see at the end of the hot day
> the flowers all withered.[34]

Love leaves a whispering note through the wind of the spring. It is time to look back and recall the happy moments of union. Is the tune of the *veena*—the tune that glorified the moments of love—lost in oblivion ? Perhaps not. The weeping *ragini* raging the early spring hours is just a reminder to join the festival of love always going on within the lover and the beloved. Love is thus eternalised in reminiscence serene and sombre in poignance. The *lovę-lost heart* is exposed as follows :

> Who whispers the tune unknown in ears
> In songs my thoughts go afloating
> In the land of the shadow of forgotten birth
> In the bereavement of the lost *veena*
> The way-lost ragini wanders weeping in the wind
> of the early spring
> In which night of union of the spring towards the
> stars
> Do my thoughts trek afloating in songs and songs.[35]

Love is always a haunting endeavour within to find out the casket of love. It is a search thrilling unending mysterious painful hilarious but bewitching. Does love step on at the midnight hours when the footprints become blessed with the agonising warmth of love ? Pain, then, finds a new language with the christening of love. The *sitar* plays on only to glorify the agonising moments of the lover and the beloved. Would anyone of the two—the lover and the beloved—remain apart ? If so, why not the inner conflict take the upper hand ? Why not the suppressed languishment of love finds its manifestation in the form of desperate violence ? And so the strings of the sitar are torn to pieces ? The music comes to an end—the music that vibrates in the long-awaiting souls of the lover and the beloved. Does the music actually end ! Does silence fail to speak within in the most profound language of love ? Perhaps not, otherwise love would be meaningless and unworthy of being remembered in moments of languishment. Even silence adorned with the conflicts of love makes a new promise of love to be rechristened in purity and magnificence.

Tagore, therefore, makes a new approach to love—altogether new, of course, - to redefine love in a purposefully purposeless manner. The song of love he sings, verges in a platonic vein but at the same time the romance of love still persists. The song of love is the song of dedication to the lover or the beloved as the case may be, and, therefore, never becomes purposeless. The yearning for the solemn union always exists and thrives in panoramic visions. The tune floats or flies like a bird. The beautiful countenance flashes all of a sudden. Like a dream of yore and in a new garb the beloved appears. Who denies such a beauty ? Who fails to recall the singing boat of the past plying along the river of reminiscence in twain ?

Love as Tagore muses on, becomes symbolic in the forms of flowers and birds. The fragrance of flowers signifies the aroma of love, and the very drowsiness in the eyes of birds indicates the passionate urge of love in a complete mood of intoxication in the silence of night. The flower that is yet to bloom on the lap of the beloved enjoys agonies of love's expectations that are fulfilled in the idle noontime hours when it speaks, as it were, like the contented lover with serene words of appreciation in blessed silence.

The flowers of love also keep the promise of love alive in expectation of the lover. The ardent waiting on the part of the beloved is always at the backdrop of pleasant flowers with their happy mood of greetings. The lover comes and smilingly strolls and flowers become happy companions in the ceremony of love. Love finds a new atmosphere of efflorescence. The dramatic askance of the lover in the words of the song of love finds an excellent exposure :

Where did he depart, friend, call on him
    Beneath the tree shall I stand encircling him
In this pleasant evening amid flowers in the garden
    today
    He'll stroll with a smile and that will I
    behold.
Stars have adorned the sky,
    Towards the south has the wind sped on
In the realm of slumber has the bird sung out
O the joyous, come with the tunes of pleasing spring
To bloom smoothness beneath the tree.[36]

The agonising expectation for fulfilment of love is intensely psychological with emotions charged and re-charged with variation of the poignance of love. Is love a lost language or a language perennial in the hearts of the lover and the beloved ? Is it a dream or a wakening or a synchronization of both ? Is it a token of detachment or that of an endearment of coming closer to each other and never to be separated even for a moment ? Tagore makes a characteristic portrayal of love in his unparalleled muse :

Day and night do I remain as if in the hope
of meeting someone I know not
So the mind is startled, the ears alert
The eyes thirsty and pining
Restless do I roam about
All the time do I think if I could come across her
I behold with a bizarre saying 'who is coming ?'
As the birds beckon in the forest of flowers.
In waking I do not see her,
With the hope of dream do I await
Lest she is visible in the backdrop of slumber
In the strings of dream shall I strip her
So much do I love her, so much do I want
her close to me.
I think she is not away from me
As if this desire would call on her
with eager emotion.[37]

Why is the flower garden so ideal a place for fulfilment of love? Is the blooming of flowers an indication of the ripe moment of the blooming of love? Perhaps so. All love has its freshness of poignance in the purity and smiling countenance of flowers. There is no vain mockery of prestige or position. Nor is there any foul play of emotion whatsoever. The flowers, the birds and the full moon—all create a lovely atmosphere to be blessed with the blessings of love. As Tagore muses on :

What a profuse blooming in the forest !
Is it fair to remain in pangs today ?

Leaving all honour and prestige afloating
Let's go to the flower garden.

The cuckoo has cooed time and again today
Yonder is the flute that plays on today.
Is it fair to remain in pangs today ?
Let sweetness kiss sweetness today.

Yonder is the bride of the heart
Adorned in the light of the moon
Is it fair to remain in pangs today ?[38]

With sweetness kissing sweetness, love creates a new wonderland in the world of human beings. The songs of love become the songs of the soul—stirring, agonising, pulslating, vibrating, thrilling, throbbing, unifying. The dangling lotuses of unison in the turbulent stream of youth remind the hours awaiting, the hours of poignance of love, when love will present the lover and the beloved with tears and tears of touching pain. Here is the canvas of love so lovely and nimble in the mournfully pleasing muse :

In the water of the stream of youth
In what a turbulent flood
Dangling the lotuses of unison are !
With the bloodred hue of shame her hidden dreams awaken.

Amid her perfumed hair
A single drop of tears adorns.
Blow slowly, O wind, slowly blow
With the touch of pain.
Fearful is my mind lest the string of twig does fall apart.
With pity unknown my eyes brim with tears.[39]

The dramatic moments of union between the lover and the beloved are perennial sources of life fulfilled in the poignant vision of love. Is love lost in parting moments ? Perhaps not. For the poet, the moments of parting are the moments of greater and more intensive nearness of the mind and the heart. The moments of parting are, again, the moments of purification of love in the fire of emotion and promise of reunion. As the muse reminds,

> Who harks ? Never do I look back.
> So many flowers bloom, so many wither,
> Alone do I sail along.
> The touch brimmed with the fountain of joy
> do I leave behind undisclosed.
> The fragrance of flowers flow aflying,
> Creepers breathe,
> Wailings spring forth in the forest.
> All of a sudden do I listen : adieu !
> Never do I look back.[40]

Love, indeed, takes us to a new country buoyant with the spirit of youth. May be that the name of the beloved is still unknown but that hardly matters in the ardent play of love. The resonance of songs is there in spring. The beckonings of flowers in laughter and tears are there, too. The southern wind still dances on the dishevelled hair of the beloved whose bangles ring with the sweet and lovely note of endearment :

> To a new country did I come—
> The broken boat sank, to the bank did I come afloating.
> What a unique hope the language of the mind unknown would make me listen
> The web of weal and woe would be woven in coloured thread !
> The resonance of new songs would ring
> With agony anew I would wander in laughter and tears.
> The beloved whose name is yet to be known
> Would adore heart with heart with the garland of flowers unknown.
> With the buoyant youth in the early spring
> All thro' the grass bangles would ring
> The southern wind would dance in the blooming almond creepers
> With restless dishevelled hair.[41]

Why not muse with the poet to make on endless journey to the country of love ?

REFERENCES

1. Tagore, Rabindranath : *Rabindra Rachanavali*, Government of West Bengal, Calcutta, 1987, Vol. IV, No. 381, p. 188. [Translated by the author.]
2. *Ibid.* No. 385 p. 189. Translated by the author.
3. *Ibid.* No. 1602 p. 611. Translated by the author.
4. *Ibid.* No. 1554. p. 595. Translated by the author.
5. *Ibid.* No. 1528. p. 585. Translated by the author.
6. *Ibid.* No. 403. p. 196. Translated by the author.
7. *Ibid.* No. 932. p. 385. Translated by the author.
8. *Ibid.* No. 1768. p. 736. Translated by the author.
9. *Ibid.* No. 1741. p. 727. Translated by the author.
10. *Ibid.* No. 130. p. 83. Translated by the author.
11. *Ibid.* No. 72. p. 52. Translated by the author.
12. *Ibid.* No. 323. p. 168. Translated by the author.
13. *Ibid.* No. 358. p. 179-180 Translated by the author.
14. *Ibid.* p. 148. Translated by the author.
15. *Ibid.* No. 65. p. 51. Translated by the author.
16. *Ibid.* p. 151. Translated by the author.
17. *Ibid.* No. 809. p. 339. Translated by the author.
18. *Ibid.* p. 152. Translated by the author.
19. *Ibid.* No. 117. p. 79. Translated by the author.
20. *Ibid.* No. 1666. p. 631. Translated by the author.
21. *Ibid.* No. 1423. p. 549. Translated by the author.
22. *Ibid.* No. 1143. p. 458. Translated by the author.

23. *Ibid*. No. 1301. p. 509. Translated by the author.
24. *Ibid*. No. 1696. p. 668. Translated by the author.
25. *Ibid*. No. 1733. p. 724. Translated by the author.
26. *Ibid*. No. 1267. p. 498. Translated by the author.
27. *Ibid*. No. 1581. p. 604. Translated by the author.
28. *Ibid*. No. 1768. p. 736. Translated by the author.
29. *Ibid*. No. 1729. p. 723. Translated by the author.
30. *Ibid*. No. 784. p. 332. Translated by the author.
31. *Ibid*. No. 1507. p. 578-579 Translated by the author.
32. *Ibid*. No. 342. p. 174. Translated by the author.
33. *Ibid*. No. 1126. p. 452. Translated by the author.
34. *Ibid*. No. 1324. p. 516. Translated by the author.
35. *Ibid*. No. 1725. p. 710. Translated by the author.
36. *Ibid*. No. 122. p. 81. Translated by the author.
37. *Ibid*. p. 156. Translated by the author.
38. *Ibid*. No. 113. p. 78. Translated by the author.
39. *Ibid*. No. 1365. p. 529. Translated by the author.
40. *Ibid*. p. 151. Translated by the author.
41. *Ibid*. No. 1639. p. 623. Translated by the author.

MASS EDUCATION : TAGOREAN GUIDELINES

Education is looking within in a chiselled and disciplined manner. It is self-crystallization to be 'men' from a man. If it fails to discover and rediscover the self within for the well-being of the greater self in and around, than it loses its very connotation.

An incomparable crusader against social ills and inconsistencies, Rabindranath Tagore makes a revolution both in thought and in action in the sphere of mass education. Deeply pained in the appalling and disastrous condition of the then society, he truly identifies the real cause of mass sufferings, mass poverty, and mass superstition. Absence of education which is, indeed, absence of self-observation as referred to above is the real cause of the absence of union of minds in the society. Apathy and ignorance have overpowered and eaten up the vitalities of both the individual and the social man. 'Apathy and ignorance' as Tagore prophetically pronounces, 'are the worst forms of bondage for man'. Allied to apathy and ignorance are the cancerous growth of mistrust and alienation between man and man that have even now consolidated their roles in a moribund, schizophrenic and passive society.

The whirlwind of sentimentalism unusually but certainly nurtured by the vanguards of reformation in the country during the pre-independent era has its worst effect in the area of education. Even when the whole nation is agog with the fire of national education, Tagore, the iconoclast, smells a rat quite justifiably like a foreseer in mass education. Who denies that as an educational revolutionary he has been terribly misinterpreted and misunderstood—thanks to our pawned and doled out intelligentsia—only to be left desolate from the mainstream of national renaissance ?

Perhaps desolation is always desirable to bring about real mass awakening. The beckoning is there from the celebrated ostracized for the freedom-zealots in spite of the fact that it even now goes abegging. But, then who else than Tagore can attune us with the sombre and vibrant call : *Ekla chalo re* (O trek alone) ?

To keep pace with the all-round development of mankind, Tagore emphasizes on the importance of involvement of every one in the society from every aspect of human excellence. That is why education, according to him, cannot but play a very pivotal role in mass awareness and mass co-operation. While making a broad-based study of the Indian society, he makes an intensive exposure of goodness and humanity so essential as components of mass awakening. When there is a cohesion between education and society, it means that there is no room either for ritualism or for dogmatism. That is why Hinduism, too, has its inmost message of coherence in renunciation of the self in order to welcome mass goodness and humanity in the right perspective of education. As Tagore succinctly spells out the genesis and objectives of the Indian society.

The change of life is development, the change of death, a reaction. In our society, too, changes are quickly taking place, but as there is an absence of conscious heart in the society, that change is verging towards reaction and analysis. None is being able to arrest it.

A new situation, new education, commotion with a new nation—these are undeniable. If we want to go on as if these are not existent, as if we push ourselves back towards three thousand years ago, then the conditions of those three thousand years would not be of any assistance to us and the flood of change now would float us away. If we do not admit the present in the plea of ancestry, the ancestors would not respond. Our ancestors are earnestly appealing to us by saying, 'save our achievement by making a treaty with the present, do not allow it to be utterly destroyed by blindly following it. Make a unison between one period and the other consciously safeguarding our chord of thinking. Otherwise the chord will by itself be distorted'.

What would have to be done ? Everyone in the country would sacrifice his own interest for the interest of the country. When the Hindu society was alive, then the limbs and arteries of the society would consider the interest of the whole body of the society to be its only interest. The king was the very part of the society : the assignment of social security and organisation was due to him. The Brahmins were engaged in glorifying and eternalizing the pure ideals of social religion in the society. Their meditation and erudition, devotion to education—all were the property of the society. As the resident is the architect of the society, every *ashram* residence was treated so glorious. To enrich that residence by means of wisdom, religion, idea and action, diverse forces of the society would earnestly act in different directions. The rules and functions of those days were not meaningless in the backdrop of those times.

—Rabindranath Tagore : *"Bharatvarsiya Samaj"* ("The Indian Society"), Rabindra-Rachanavali, Government of West Bengal, Calcutta, Tagore Birth Centenary Edition, 1961, Vol. XII, p. 682.

Banking upon the Indian social philosophy of ancient times from the point of view of mass education, Tagore makes a living analysis of the society at present where the education of Hindu civilization based on the promotion of goodness makes an inner revelation. The core of humanity as he ardently refers to is entirely related to the dissemination of the spirit of goodness between man and man. The 'selfless string of goodness' is the most desirable and effective string to encompass everyone in the society with the education of communicated and altruistic pattern of living. As Tagore continues,

> Now those rules are there, but that consciousness remains absent. There is not that endeavour in its limbs and arteries, keeping an eye to the well-being of the society. If we re-establish that eternally alive idea of goodness of our ancestors in our hearts as our living component and apply that in every sphere of our society, then we will be able to attain the vast Hindu civilization. It is our own duty to educate the society and provide it with health, food, wealth and money. Therein lies our goódness. Not to visualize it as a business but it is the only accomplishment not to hope *sans* virtue and goodness in exchange for that. That is union of action with the Supreme. To continually recall that is Hinduism. Instead of placing the ideal of the self at the centre of the human society, to observe it in the midst of the Brahma is in Hinduism. As a consequence, the idea of goodness towards all, from the beast to every human being, is diverged and to renunciate the self with constant practice becomes as easy as breathing. To tie every one of the society from top to bottom with a large selfless string of goodness—this alone is the bigger endeavour than all other efforts of ours. With the string of unity, the unison of religion should be made between the present and the past, between one and the other of the Hindu community. This is the only way for us to attain humanity.
>
> —*Ibid*. p. 683.

For a certain sense of revival of goodness among the masses in the society, education, as Tagore rightly points out, cannot but undertake a pivotal role. What he wants to be assured through education in the society is to bring forth mass awareness by means of revival of ancient Indian tradition in dissemination of mass education through *yatra, kathakata panchali gaan, kabi gaan, tarja, Ramayana gaan* etc. which highlight social cohesion and all round integration.

That education should never be compartmentalised and limited to a particular section of people or society but should have its involvements all over the country is undeniable. Tagore explains this truth again and again to emphasize the real role of education for mass awareness and advises on dissemination of indigenous education for mass consciousness as a positive guideline for advancement of education and society. As he characteristically remarks,

> The lofty lantern has been hung for the light of education in schools and colleges, but if that is a captured light in the closed walls, then we would say that we are unfortunate. A picture manifests throughout the canvas. Likewise, in order to have explicity, education awaits countrywide involvement. That education bereft of its extensive role is so vague and incomplete, it pains of poverty have died down in our mind due to our habits alone. When we compare our country with the other one on education, we only observe the visible part and never make an account of the invisible one. With resemblance, we see there are also universities there, and their replicas in the forms of one or two are also being seen in our country. We forget that there is not a single fortunate country where beyond the stipulated educational institutions there is not a wider circumference well spread throughout the horizon of nonstipulated education embracing the whole society.
>
> — Rabindranath Tagore : *"Sikshar Vikiran"* "Dissemination of Education"), *Siksha*, Visva-Bharati, 1973, p. 214.

Synchronization of education with ancient culture and tradition is enrichment of education in the right perspective of mass consciousness. Tagore wants to redirect education towards revival of age old culture and tradition of India, which would enable everyone in the society to exercise mental abilities in the most worthwhile manner. A certain sense of introspective involvement by means of such kind of mass education would certainly bring forth desirable revolution in the sphere of mass education. Tagore elucidates this point as follows :

> Like the mediaeval era of Europe, education through the *sastras* alone was fundamental. The special pursuit of this education was made in *toles, chatuspathis* but the role of learning was extended through out the country. There was a continual exchange between specialized knowledge and general knowledge. There was not that antagonistic relationship between the assembly of scholars and unscholarly locality as between an oasis and a desert. There was no part in the country that did not endear the *Ramayana*, the *Mahabharata*, the religious discourses that would regularly spread through diverse channels. Even those theoretical knowledge that are discussed under strenuous perseverance in philosophy were also irrigated in the soil of the minds of the masses all the time. The food for the tree needs to be made liquid so that the tree might take it in all its branches and twigs. In the same way, serious learning in those days has been simplified and disseminated among the minds of the masses. When public work was a part of religion in our country, the arrangements for reservoirs of water at every village were extensive by nature. To quench thirst, arrangements for water were spontaneously made by all together. There was no need for appearing to the spend-thrift personnels of the royal court for water. In the same way, society has disseminated indigenous learning

> in spontaneity. Otherwise, the whole country would turn into cruelly black barbarities. Learning, then, was not a property of the learned. That was a property of the whole society.
>
> —*Ibid.*, p. 214-215

Even when education is doled out in abstraction in schools, colleges and universities in our country and a sense of apathy and indignity still persists more or less in our system, Tagore reminds us of a few illustrious mass educators of our country whose contributions towards education for social awareness are based on the Indian perspective of altruism : *a no bhadra kratava yantu visvatah*—let noble thoughts come to us from all sides. Education for liberation of intellect is the pre-requisite for dissemination of education and if our educational institutions fail to impart that spirit of education for mass consciousness, let there be no schools, colleges, universities or any other altar of learning. That life appropriately and communicatingly lived in fulness is what education should always cater to, and if this is not possible through education, let there be no education at all. Tagore makes a fine analysis on this point, which deserves special attention right now :

> That education is true, which acknowledges the mind to be a living thing, and therefore stimulates it to give out more in quality and quantity than is imparted to it from outside. And we are to judge our education by that standard.
>
> Therefore, the question is : whether, in our intellectual career in the modern time, we have given more than we have received, and created something which is our own. For when any race of men becomes a mere burden in the world, rendering no satisfactory account of the cost it imposes upon the society, this, for it, is worse than death. For this is the intolerably mean situation of remaining under the charge of perpetual misappropriation.
>
> As for us, far from having given our university more than we received, we have not even rendered back in full measure. We have been repeating great words, learning great truths,

looking on great examples, but, in turn, we have simply become clerks, deputy magistrates, pleaders or physicians.

Not that it is a small thing to be, for instance, a physician. But though our physicians are now practising in every town and village and hamlet of the country and though many of them are of good repute and making money, all this extensive experience of theirs has not resulted in any new theory, or great fact, being added to the science of medicine. Like good school-boys, they have only applied with over-cautious precision just what they have learnt. And who shall make good the vital thing that is lost when students never become masters ?

Yet I cannot admit that this is due to any inherent defect in our natural power. There was a long period in the past, during which the science of healing with us was a living growth, spreading its different off-shoots and branches all over our country. That teaches us at least this much that in those days our mind was in living connection with its acquirements; that, then, we did not merely learn by rote, but made our own observations and experiments; that we tried to discover principles and build hypotheses and apply them to life.

Where has this initiative and courage of ours have departed ? Why do we tread so carefully, so fearfully under the load of our learning ? Is it because we were born to be serfs, permanently bending under the burden of another's intellectual acquisitions ? Never !

For even in spite of the scarcity of opportunities and narrowness of prospects, in spite of our present defective education, which has been starved of all life elements, a few great men of science like Jagadishchandra and Prafullachandra, and a great scholar like Brajendranath have made their appearance in our country, proving that the power of true originality is not lacking among our people; only it is trampled down under the dead pressure of a mechanical method and the callousness of contemptuous discouragement.

— Rabindranath Tagore : *The Centre of Indian Culture*, Visva-Bharati Book Shop, Calcutta, 1951, p. 9-11.

The spontaneous growth of man through mass education has the inherent objective of understanding and appreciating the traditional approaches to dissemination of education among all the people of the society. In order to revive and accentuate indigenous education, Tagore draws our attention towards mutual exchange of ideas and experiences that takes place in the occasional indigenous social congregations like the *melas*, the *yatras* and so on, which greatly contribute to spread of mass education. Moreover, the education of self-esteem, self-development and self-study so essential for fullness of man and total development of personality is derived through enrichment of mass education in the indigenous society.

Tagore, therefore, insists on dealing with mass education at the grass-root level of the rural society where education still awaits its adequate and appropriate dissemination. If the rural people living in the rural society are properly and carefully stimulated in self-askance, self-enquiry and self-development with the help of indigenous education, the real purpose of education of being will be definitely fulfilled. Such type of mass education indigenous, and, therefore, rooted to the soil, would certainly enkindle the spirit of patriotism in undertaking and appreciating social responsibilities so sadly lacking in stereotyped formal education that only caters to bare livelihood.

A rejuvenated interest in mass education for rural reconstruction as Tagore introduces in his programme for rural development is to bring about a certain sense of social consciousness which alone makes a healthy ground of synchronization between man and man. In his delineation with the *swadeshi samaj* or indigenous society, he harps on the importance of mas education in accordance with the guidelines that even now serve as pointers to education of the masses from the right perspectives :

> Our country is primarily rural oriented. When these villages become enthusiastic now and then to feel in their pulses the blood circulation of the big

world outside, then fairs alone are the way out. These fairs beckon the outer world inside, in these festivals, villages become free from all pettiness : this is the fundamental scope for contributing whole-heartedly and for accepting others. As the advent of the rains is to fill in the tanks with the water from the sky, so the appropriate scope for filling in the hearts of the villages is the fair.

This fair is very natural in our country. If you call on the countrymen in connection with a meeting, they will attend fearfully; it will take a long time to open out their minds. But when all congregate together on the occasion of a fair, they easily come with open hearts. And so the real scope to win the minds of the country becomes available. When the villagers have taken leave by discontinuing cultivation, then alone is the time to sit beside them.

There is not a single district in Bengal where in the different periods of the year and at different places fairs are not held. First, it is our duty to collect a list and an account of these fairs. Afterwards we should take records to be rightly acquainted with the people of the country in connection with these fairs.

In every district, the gentle and educated community can awaken their fairs anew and invigorate in new hearts afresh, if the educated persons of the country infuse their hearts into these fairs, if they establish good relationship among the Hindus and the Muslims in these fairs, make consultations for eradicating the lacuna of the district in relation to schools, conveyance, tanks, cultivated lands etc. leaving off all connections with barren politics; then, within a very short

> time, they can really turn out the country to be dynamic.
>
> — Rabindranath Tagore : *"Swadeshi Samaj", Rabindra Rachanavali,* Government of West Bengal, Calcutta, Tagore Birth Centenary Edition, 1961, Vol. XII, p. 688.
>
> [Translated by the author]

The education for life which is the genesis of the education of being is what is to be derived through mass education. To be true to this objective, Tagore refers to the fundamental guideline for mass education in bringing about a positive change of approach to life in launching a newer adventure in mutual understanding between man and man. That the global human society is acting from the ailings of dissociation and disunity terribly backed by apathy and ignorance should be the primary target of challenge in war footing. Therefore, Tagore's guidelines for mass education has a global approach which necessitates immediate re-thinking and re-evaluating in our approach to mass education right now or never. A synchronization of the little man caged and cornered in a little society with man the legion striving towards realization of the global society is, indeed, the need of the hour. The rediscovery of humanity in man by means of mass education is the rediscovery of global civilization. As Tagore reminds us,

> Man is to win his humanity at every moment. The history of every nation is the history of its own march for victory. Its health and its wealth lie in eliminating difficult obstacles. For this, it is said : fortune favours the brave. Man has made the inaccessible accessible and unattainable attainable. A particular nation as it is involved in a particular problem by the Almighty, finds it out in giving true reply to it. Those who have failed to solve are undone. And those who have thought that there is nothing to solve and every thing has

> been solved have alone become distressed. So long as there is life in man there are problems for him. His process of living is to ceaselessly give answers to problems. All around there are continual constraints of the non-living. To continually challenge these constraints is to prove that life is. * * * * The fundamental principle of the human society is the unity of man. Civilization means practice of mankind to be united. Wherever the realization of this theory of unity is weak, the country is entangled with that weakness in forms of manifold diseases and is attacked from all around.
>
> — Rabindranath Tagore : *"Bharatpathik Rammohan Roy"*, *Rabindra-Rachanavali*, Government of West Bengal, Calcutta, Tagore Birth Centenary Edition, 1961, Vol. XI, p. 384.
>
> [Translated by the author]

To 'know man and to make oneself known to man', as Tagore highlights in his philosophy of mass education should be the eternal guideline in our strategy of education for human development. True education for awakening of mass conciousness and humanism deserves our renewed approach to education to understand the language of personality over and above that of intellect. A 'dead load of dumb wisdom' as he categorically points out, must be replaced by an ever-growing sense of appreciation to art and culture and to other finer sensibilities and softer visions of life. Mass education should, therefore, be steered towards understanding and appreciation of art and aesthetics with renewed interest and attention.

With the above ends in view of mass education as living education with particular devotion to art and aesthetics, Tagore categorically analyses the role of education as follows :

The great use of Education is not merely to collect facts, but to know man and make oneself known to man. It is the duty of every human being to master, at least to some extent, not only the language of intellect but also that of personality which is the language of Art. It is a great world of reality for man —vast and profound —this growing world of his own creative nature. This is the world of Art. To be brought up in ignorance of it is to be deprived of the knowledge and use of that great inheritance of humanity, which has been growing and waiting for every one of us from the beginning of our history. It is to remain deaf to the eternal voice of Man, that just speaks to all men the messages that are beyond speech. From the educational point of view we know Europe where it is scientific, or at best literary. So our notion of its modern culture is limited within the boundary lines of grammar and the laboratory. We almost completely ignore the aesthetic life of man, leaving it uncultivated, allowing weeds to grow there. Our newspapers are prolific, our meeting places are vociferous; and in them we wear to shred the things we have borrowed from our English teachers. We make the air dismal and damp with the tears of our grievances. But where are our arts, which, like the outbreak of spring flowers, are the spontaneous overflow of our deeper nature and spiritual magnificence ?

Through this great deficiency of our modern education, we are condemned to carry to the end a dead load of dumb wisdom. Like Miserable outcasts, we are deprived of our place in the festival of culture, and wait at the outer court, where the colours are not for us, nor the forms of delight, nor the songs. Ours is the education of a prison-house, with hard labour and with a drab dress cut to the limits of minimum decency and

> necessity. We are made to forget that the perfection of colour and form and expression belongs to the perfection of vitality,—that the joy of life is only the other side of the strength of life. The timber merchant may think that the flowers and foliage are mere frivolous decorations of a tree; but if these are suppressed, he will know to his cost that the timber too will fail.
>
> — Rabindranath Tagore : "An Eastern University", *Creative Unity,* Macmillan & Company Limited, London, 1962, p. 196-98.

For a re-orientation of education in the indigenous pattern, Tagore specially emphasizes on unification of education with life—a fact which he highlights in his seminal treatise *"Sikshar Herpher"* ("Topsy-turvy in Education")—because he firmly believes that regeneration man by means of mass education essentially depends on indigenous education which becomes living and pulsating. As such education is rooted to the soil, education for fulness becomes a reality from every point of view.[1]

The inner heart of the society, as Tagore firmly believes and actualizes in practice of perfection, must be revived through mass education. For this, a living and dynamic approach to the positive aspects of social reconstruction should be closely related to the indigenous strategies for dissemination of mass education. He, therefore, gives special emphasis on education through the mother-tongue which becomes very favourable for negotiating this particular end in view of mass education. As he categorically observes,

> If we admit to win the heart of the society as the highest attainment, then the activities to which we have already been accustomed in ordinary mode of living should be kept apart and the avenues that are eternally open for

> approaching the country in reality should be brought to light before us. Suppose, if we appoint our provincial conference to the indigenous strategies in reality, then what would we do ? Then, instead of arranging a meeting in the foreign pattern, we would have arranged a meeting of the indigenous one. There the people of the country would congregate from distant places in *Yatras*, songs, festivals and entertainment. An exhibition of indigenous commodities and agricultural products would take place there. Good performers of *Kathak*, *Kirtan* singers and teams of *Yatra* performers would be rewarded there. The masses would be advised on theories of health and hygiene through magic lanterns etc. there and whatever we would like to say, whatever we would like to advise on weal and woe would have been discussed together irrespective of persons gentle or not, in simple Bengali language.
>
> — Rabindranath Tagore : *"Swadeshi Samaj"* ("The Indigenous Society"), Rabindra-Rachanavali, Government of West Bengal, Calcutta, Tagore Birth Centenary Edition, 1961, Vol. XII, p. 687-88.
>
> [Translated by the author]

To reintroduce *ashramic* education as a strategy for education for all in a harmonized atmosphere where the spirit of oneness is best felt and realized, Tagore reminds us that our entire endeavour towards intellectual education should be replaced by education for sympathy along with spiritual and physical education. This will bring man closer to man in the society. Let education be vibrant with manifold activities that amply contribute to mass awareness and mass contact. Let it be so pursued as to awaken the inner spirit of mankind.[2]

The most living perspective of mass education as Tagore rightly asserts is education of the living mind for a living global vision of man. The education of the *ashram* as he has thought and experimented upon in his own educational institution at Santiniketan is the cultivation of curiosity and refinement of vision spreading beyond bookish knowledge. As he profoundly observes,

> It is absence of curiosity that indicates the passivity of the mind. Today the nations dominating over the world have exhibited their indomitable curiosity upon everything of this world. There is neither any country nor any time nor, again, any subject towards which their mind is not being thrust forward. This living power of mind on their part came out victorious throughout the world.
>
> *   *   *   *   *
>
> The education of the *ashram* is to live in fulness. One can ascend the highest peak of the first class in the examination even with a dead mind. We are regularly accustomed to this fact in our country. It is seen that the very good students of the college secure titles of honour but never secure the world. From the very beginning, I had the resolution that the boys of the *ashram* would remain curious of having immediate relations all around. They will seek, examine and collect Here teachers whose visions spread beyond the horizon of books would assemble.
>
> — Rabindranath Tagore : *"Ashramer Siksha"*, *Siksha*, Visva-Bharati, 1973, p. 48-49

[Translated by the author]

Mass education should also be guided towards education for a sound body in order to have a sound mind. When Tagore launches a crusade against social superstitions with regard to health and hygiene in the rural societies, he specifically wants to eradicate the prevailing ailing condition of the societies where people suffer from numerous physical and mental illness. In fact, eradication of malaria, renovation of ponds, wells, canals etc., arrangement for adequate supply of pure drinking water, the training of rural people against natural calamities diseases and accidents like flood, fire, epidemics etc. and awareness to social superstitions related to health and hygiene are the regular programmes of education for rural development and rural reconstruction that were undertaken by the devoted followers of Tagorean education for mass consciousness in the earlier decades of the twentieth century in and around Sriniketan, Visva-Bharati, West Bengal.

Awareness to physical education as an inseparable part of mass education as propounded by Tagore has its indigenous avenues of emancipation in the introduction of games and sports. Drills, exercises, wrestling, boxing, knife-play, stick-play, etc. are regular items of physical education side by side with training in western folk sports, games and items of physical fitness such as Irish dance, wand dance etc. What Tagore wants to highlight in course of introducing all these programmes of physical education is to train in the art of self-development, self-defence, self-growth and self-awareness side by side with training in socio-creative and socio-co-operative endeavour. The introduction of *brati-balaks* and *brati-balikas* in the pattern of boys' scouts and girls' guides is a genuine example of how Tagore steers mass education in the society towards a well-disciplined, well-guided, well-thought out programme of education for emergence of fulness in man.

Synchronization of creativity and freedom is another invaluable guideline for mass education that Tagore time and again reminds us. Unless mass education is enriched with creativity, it merges into a utilitarian and commercial approach to education from which traditional pattern of education terribly suffers even now. To create a suitable and comprehensive atmosphere of advancement of learning even in the non-formal pattern of education incorporated in the adult education programmes is not only desirable but also mandatory. As such, Tagore introduces the *Loka-siksha Samsad* (The Institute of Mass Education) where courses of studies are closely oriented with the diverse patterns of life of the masses—their hopes, anxieties, happiness, poverty, sufferings etc.—and where the books are so written as to be easily read, understood and appreciated by the masses. It is interesting to note that in this great endeavour, Tagore has been able to draw the attention of the learned scholars, distinguished experts in different disciplines and eminent persons in all walks of life and the society to write simple, easy-to-read books on different subjects. Persons like Acharya Bidhu Sekhar Shastri, Ajit Chakraborty, Jagadishchandra Bose, Prasantachandra Mahalanabish, Kshitimohan Sen, Haricharan Bandyopadhyay, U.N. Brahmachari, Nityananda Vinode Goswamy and many others have spontaneously responded to his invitation to write books on science, literature, physics, oriental studies, astronomy, statistics, medical science etc. for dissemination of education among the masses in a well-planned manner.

Apart from the constructive approach to education for the masses to bring about a sense of self-esteem and self-reliance, Tagore stimulates aesthetic education as an indivisible part of mass education. This is because he sincerely believes that all education should be geared to the fulness of growth and personality for which the education of Truth, Goodness and Beauty should always be exercised with all care and caution.

Religion, too, forms an essential part in Tagore's guidelines to mass education. Religion, of course, has an altogether different end in view from what is normally conceived, for Tagore synchronizes religion with education in the discovery of the true religion of man. It is that religion which enshrines the value of the inner man, the man divine liberated from apathy, ignorance, intolerance, and all other forms of narrowness of mind. Again, when Tagore harmonizes between religion and education, he shows us the avenue of excellence of the eternal spirit of *atman*—the spirit of the Self Eternal.

Do we strive to direct mass education now towards emancipation and excellence of the Self Eternal in Man ?

NOTES AND REFERENCES

1. S. Radhakrishnan makes characteristic references to Tagore's principles and guidelines of dissemination of mass education in conformity with indigenous education based on the *ashramic* pattern as follows :

   The ideal which India possessed in the past should come back in its essence, though not in its entirety. "The highest education is that which does not merely give us information but makes our life in harmony with all existence." (*The Spirit of Japan,* p. 116). The object of education is to give man the unity of truth. Formerly when life was simple, all the different elements of man were in complete harmony. But when there came the separation of the intellect from the spiritual and the physical, the school education put entire emphasis on intellectual and the physical side of man. We devote our sole attention in giving children information, not knowing that by this emphasis we are accentuating a break between the intellectual, physical, and the spiritual life. (*Ibid.* p. 126). But how is the spiritual life to be cultivated ? Not by means of any set of lessons about God and His existence but by allowing the souls to express themselves freely and spontaneously. Rabindranath trusts the instinct of the pupil and the atmosphere of the *ashram* for the kindling of the spiritual aspiration and the development of the spiritual life. "With the breath we draw we must always feel the truth, that we are living in God" (*Ibid*). In ancient India it was possible, because in the *ashram* which is home, school, temple and forest rolled into one, the teachers were men who every moment felt the presence of God and lived their life to Him. So their pupils felt God as they felt the green of the earth or the blue of the sky. Education, which aims at the emancipation of the soul and the liberation of the human spirit from its trammels, would open the eyes of Indians to the enormous waste of time, health and spirit, which daily takes place in the country; would reveal to them the complete circumscription of opportunity, and would give them the courage of heart and strength of mind to fight injustice in every form. In this school at Bolpur, which is not only a school of culture but an abode of piety and a school of art, Rabindranath combines modern methods of education with the ancient Indian ideal of soul-culture. To him the ideal school "must be an ashram where men have gathered together for the highest end of life, in the peace of nature; where life is not merely meditative but fully awake in its activities, where boys' minds are not perpetually drilled into believing that the ideal of the self-idolatry of the nation is the truest ideal for them to accept; where they are bidden to realise man's world as God's kingdom to whose citizenship they have to aspire; where the sunrise and sunset and the silent glory of the stars are not daily ignored; where nature's festivities of flowers and fruit have their joyous recognition from man; and where the young and the old, the teacher and the student sit at the same table to partake of their daily food and the food of their eternal life." (*Ibid.* p. 148)

— S. Radhakrishnan : *The Philosophy of Rabindranath Tagore,* Good Companions Publishers, Baroda, India, 1961, p. 127-28.

2. In *"Ashramer siksha"* ("The Education of the Ashram"), Tagore emphasizes on education that infuses in every pupil 'to live in fulness'. This has its practical revelation in his own school *Siksha-Satra* (*The Poet's School*) where education caters to the training of the right mind of awareness to one and all. Elmhirst, a devoted and close associate of Tagore in his programme for mass education,

describes the educational activities of Siksha-Satra as follows :

Records are kept and reports and accounts are written up, revised and corrected giving scope for literary training in its most interesting form. Geology becomes the fertility of the plot; chemistry the use of lime and manures of all kinds of spray and disinfectants; physics the use of tools, pumps, the study of water-lift and oil engines; entomology and control of plant pests (ants, cater-pillars, bettles) and diseases (leaf curl, wilt, bacterial attacks); orinthology, the study of birds in their relation first to the garden plot and to the world in general.

There is no room in Siksha-Satra for Nature-study as an abstract subject, divorced from life and the needs of life. In life the child has to face the mosquito mightily, perhaps the bug or flea, the bacterial of typhoid, of cholera, of small-pox as well as forces of nature which attack his trees, his plants, and his livestock. Nature-study is thus transformed into the study of nature in relation to life and daily experiences of life.

— L.K. Elmhirst : *Rabindranath Tagore : Pioneer in Education*, John Murry, London, 1961, p. 73-74.

THE MYSTIC VISION OF TAGORE IN GITANJALI

Mysticism, a journey *par excellence* from being to the beyonding of being, is the truest image of man. It is the vision of man in unending crystallization of consciousness—*cha vai tu hi*—thou art that—the unison of the being with the ever abiding All Beautiful.

Myopic as man is in the mystic vision of beings. Rabindranath Tagore, the mystic visionary unique and unparalleled, shows us the inner avenues of mystic fulfilment. The journey to the beyonding of man appears in all dimensions of poignance and freshness. The poignance, again, appears in the diverse patterns of perfumes of promise, and freshness leaves behind the aroma of excellence in limitless endeavour.

Who act as components of mystic perfumes of promise and poignance ? Who steer man to the prized excellence of perfection ? For Tagore, the answers are simple but indubitably unacceptable by a myopic mesmerized in macabre abstractions of automation. And so, when the eerie silence all around prepares the battered mind for the mystic moments of fulness of vision, the prayer for the All Beautiful presents us with an ever-living and radiant imagery :

> If thou speakest not I will fill my heart with thy silence and endure it. I will keep still and wait like the night with starry vigil and its head bent low with patience.
>
> The morning will surely come, the darkness will vanish, and thy voice pour down in golden streams breaking through the sky.
>
> Then thy words will take wing in songs from every one of my birds' nests, and thy melodies will break forth in flowers in all my forest groves.[1]

The melodies of the All Beautiful bringing forth a new world of serenity and consciousness of being are the fountains of eternal joy. For Tagore, man haunts for that joy everlasting in the stream of consciousness. Forced as every human being is to negotiate the trammels and weariness of life, the succour must be found out. But how ? It is to surrender to the All Preserver wholeheartedly to protect the being against falling in line with the stereo-typed process of defence : struggle, struggle, and struggle. Is struggle better than looking within for a look anew ? Is it more vibrant than the language of trust upon the Supreme Being awaiting welcome in worship ? For 'a fresher gladness of awakening', Tagore, therefore, is firm in his conviction that the veil of night is the veil of awakening for a better day to come :

> In the night of weariness let me give myself up to sleep without struggle, resting my trust upon thee.
>
> Let me not force my flagging spirit into a poor preparation for thy worship.
>
> It is thou who drawest the veil of night upon the tired eyes of the day to renew its sight in a fresher gladness of awakening.[2]

To be in tune with the All Beautiful is to bring back the inner essence of life—the essence of the beyonding of man. It is the lost music of the inner man that frantically seeks unison with that of the All Beautiful. That music is like a holy stream. With a baffled voice as Tagore humbly admits, the song mystic and divine is yet to be sung. The sense of amazement weaves a web of humble submission like a captive, around the music of the Supreme Singer :

> I know not how thou singest, my master !
> I ever listen in silent amazement.
>
> The light of thy music illumines the world. The life breath of thy music runs from sky to sky. The holy stream of thy music breaks through all stony obstacles and rushes on.
>
> My heart longs to join in thy song, but vainly struggles for a voice. I would speak, but speech breaks not into song, and I cry out baffled. Ah, thou hast made my heart captive in the endless meshes of thy music, my master ![3]

Is the master's call for the beyonding of being reaches the ears of man bound in the shackles of indulgence ? How are the shackles entangled ? How is the being in sheer delight of unison with the All Serene ? The worthier moments of life often prove failures in poignance of serenity. The blessedness of beyonding remains a myth with the absence of the consoling spurt of the Holy Grail. The invitation is there—always and eternal—from the world of Nature to the world of man. Is gladness the antidote to the miseries of the inner man ? Perhaps it is a component for renewal of vision—the vision from outer affluence to inner grandeur—the grandeur of serenity. A true mystic cannot but pine for that prized serenity. A look within with a quiet mind refreshed in the fountain of 'sighs and murmurs' and abundance of songs of adoration is a look for the recrystallization of the mind to be prepared for the serene encounter with the matchless mystic :

> I ask for a moment's indulgence to sit by thy side. The works that I have in hand I will finish afterwards.

> Away from the sight of thy face my heart knows no rest or respite, and my work becomes an endless toil in a shoreless sea of toil.
>
> Today the summer has come at my window with its sighs and murmur; and the bees are plying their minstrelsy at the court of the flowering grove.
>
> Now it is time to sit quiet, face to face in this silent and overflowing nature.[4]

To sit face to face with the All Beautiful in an atmosphere quiet and serene is to be enriched with the awe and wonder the heart so gravely pines for. To sit face to face with Him is to be blessed with the prized moment of beyonding. Does the moment really come ? Or is it a fancy the poet adorns rather romantically ? For Tagore, the reality of the All Beautiful is beyond doubt. Who but a serene mystic radiant with the aura of the All Beautiful can present us with a dramatic situation in words of music as follows ?

> He came and sat by my side but I work not. What a cursed sleep it was, O miserable me !
>
> He came when the night was still; he had his harp in his hands, and my dream became resonant with its melodies.
>
> Alas, why are my nights all thus lost ? Ah, why do I ever miss his sight whose breath touches my sleep ?[5]

The desires of the heart for such an encounter with the All Beautiful are, however, a forewarning in mystic inconsistencies. The 'perils of the weak' should be negotiated by refusals. Hurriedness in mystic vision is simply a sign of failure to reach the ultimate objective—the mystic fulfilment and unison with the All Beautiful. Tagore is aware of such inconsistencies in his mystic endeavour, and so he frankly admits his pitfalls and gratefully acknowledges the refusal :

> Day by day thou art making me worthy of the simple, great gifts that thou gavest to me unasked—this sky and the light, this body and the life and the mind—saving me from perils of overmuch desire.
>
> There are times when I languidly linger and times when I awaken and hurry in search of my goal; but cruelly thou hidest thyself from before me.
>
> Day by day thou art making me worthy of thy full acceptance by refusing me over and anon, saving me from perils of weak, uncertain desire.[6]

To be seasoned in mystic vision in the pitfalls of unworthiness is a great lesson for a luminous mystic visionary. Tagore searches for the inwardness of that mystic vision in the joy of being alone in the world of affluence of beauty. He is enamoured with such beauty as we find in his mystic experience of the lord of thunder. The terrible halo of beauty in the wristlet adorned with stars and multi-coloured jewels makes a poorer show than the curved halo of light beaming forth from the sword of thunder. The mystic askance obviously surpasses all earthly experiences : Is the ecstasy of pain not a pre-condition to purity of vision kissed by the flash of lightning from the curve of the sword ? Here is a panoramic vision of mystic fulfilment :

> Beautiful is thy wristlet, decked with stars and cunningly wrought in myriad-coloured jewels. But more beautiful to me thy sword with its curve of lightning like the outspread wings of the divine bird of Vishnu, perfectly poised in the angry red light of the sunset.
>
> It quivers like the one last response of life in ecstasy of pain at the final stroke of death; it shines like the pure flame of being burning up earthly sense with one fierce flash.

> Beautiful is thy wristlet, decked with starry gems; but thy sword, O lord of thunder, is wrought with uttermost beauty, terrible to behold or to think of.[7]

An example of prayer and mystic vision, the above muse of Rabindranath comes closer to Sri Aurobindo who glorifies the voice of the essential man in the mystic crescendo as we find in "Rose of God".

> Rose of God, vermilion stain on the sapphires of heaven,
> Rose of Bliss, fire-sweet, seven-tinged with the ecstasies seven !
> Leap up in the heart of humanhood, O miracle, O flame,
> Passion-flower of the Nameless, bud of the mystical Name.
>
> Rose of God, great wisdom-bloom on the summits of being,
> Rose of Light, immaculate core of the ultimate seeing !
> Live in the mind of our earthhood, O golden Mystery, flower
> Sun on the head of the Timeless, guest of the marvellous Hour.
>
> Rose of God, demask force of Infinity, red icon of might,
> Rose of Power, with thy diamond halo piercing the night !
> Ablaze in the will of the mortal, design the wonder of the plan,
> Image of Immortality, outbreak of the Godhead in man.
>
> Rose of God, smitten purple with the incarnate divine Desire,
> Rose of Life, crowded with petals, colours' lyre !
> Transform the body of the mortal like a sweet and magical rhyme ;

Bridge our earthhood and heavenhood, make
deathless the children of Time.

Rose of God, like a blush of rapture on Eternity's
face,

Rose of love, ruby depth of all being, fire-passion of
Grace !

Arise from the heart of yearning that sobs in
Nature's abyss :

Make earth the home of the Wonderful and life
Beatitude's kiss.[8]

To 'bridge over earthhood and heavenhood' Tagore also delves deep into the wonderland of mystic poignance. To him, the heart of yearning is the heart of 'calm of mind, all passions spent'. For a journey unending, he never looks behind, but looks ahead like a child ever graceful with the grace of the All Serene.

To be a playmate with children 'on the sea shore of worlds' as Tagore portrays by means of his inward vision of mystic delight is to feel the presence of the All Beautiful. Then the worldly attraction becomes meaningless like the houses with sands on the sea-shores. On the threshold of desirable preparation to encounter the Comrade Eternal, passion is purified like empty shells and withered leaves. Pomp and vainglory are replaced by the profoundness of freedom from all material abstractions. The time is ripe for mystic fulfilment, since it becomes deathless and the mind is well prepared to cast the net of mystic beyonding. The canvas of such a mystic beyonding of consciousness as Tagore sets before us is significant :

On the seashore of endless worlds children meet. The infinite sky is motionless overhead and the restless water is boisterous. On the seashore of endless worlds the children meet with shouts and dances.

They build their houses with sand and they play with empty shells. With withered leaves they

> weave their boats and smilingly float them on the vast deep. Children have their play on the seashore of worlds.
>
> They know not how to swim, they know not how to cast nets. Pearl fishers dive for pearls, merchants sail in their ships, while children gather pebbles and scatter them again. They seek not for hidden treasures, they know not how to cast nets.[9]

The mystic vision of light as Tagore elucidates in *Gitanjali* is an unparalleled strategy for the beyonding of man. Dismayed by sufferings and darkness of ignorance and torn between yearnings and perfection man is ever scornful of himself for his limitations to encounter the All Beautiful. Tagore shows a new avenue of self-preparation and boosts the morale of the baffled self to enkindle 'the lamp of love' that will promise life with the perfume of the mystic fragrance of fulfilment. As he bursts forth with musical resonance in an emotion-soaked soliloquy,

> Light, oh where is the light ? Kindle it with the burning fire of desire !
>
> There is the lamp but never a flicker of a flame—is such thy fate, my heart ? Ah, death were better by far for thee !
>
> Misery knocks at thy door, and her message is that thy lord is wakeful, and he calls thee to the love-tryst through the darkness of night.
>
> The sky is overcast with clouds and the rain is ceaseless, I know not what this is that stirs in me—I know not its meaning.
>
> A moment's flash of lightning drags down a deeper gloom on my sight, and my heart gropes for the path to where the music of the night calls me.
>
> Light, oh where is the light ! Kindle it with the burning fire of desire ! It thunders and the wind rushes screaming through the void. The night is

> black as a black stone. Let not the hours pass by in the dark. Kindle the lamp of love with thy life.[10]

Elsewhere, Tagore asserts that light alone will bring about the moment of ecstasy—the moment when the depth of unconsciousness rings with the cry of unison with the All Beautiful.

The moment of the Great Encounter is also clear and specific to the mystic visionary. The aching heart knows well when the All Holy and All Wakeful will grace His serene presence with light and thunder. As Tagore muses in the mystic tune,

> When the heart is hard and parched up, come upon me with the shower of mercy. When grace is lost from life, come with a burst of song.
>
> When tumultuous work raises its din on all sides shutting me out from beyond, come to me, my lord of silence, with thy peace and rest.
>
> When my beggarly heart sits crouched, shut up in a corner, break open the door, my king, and come with the ceremony of a king.
>
> When desire blinds the mind with delusion and dust, O thou holy one, thou wakeful, come with thy light and thy thunder.[11]

Waiting for the All Beautiful is waiting for the great splendour of light. For Tagore it is a moment of mystic askance. Where is the All Enkindler ? Does He wait on the timeless hours of silence leaving behind 'all glamour of glory' ? Should the poet wait for Him in vain ? Here is a frank confession crystallized in mystic agony :

> I sit on the grass and gaze upon the sky and dream of the sudden splendour of thy coming—all the lights ablaze, golden pennons flying over the car, and they at the roadside standing agape, when they see thee come down from thy seat to raise me from the dust, and set at thy side this ragged

> beggar girl a-tremble with shame and pride, like a creeper in a summer breeze.
>
> But time glides on and still no sound of the wheels of thy chariot. Many a procession passes by with noise and shouts and glamour of glory. It is only thou who wouldst stand in the shadow silent and behind them all ? And only I who would wait and weep and wear out my heart in vain longing ?[12]

Silence speaks in a language most mystic and serene to the All Beautiful. This is a great mystic experience that Tagore feels in the inmost core of his heart. To encounter the King of kings, it is better to be alone, for he knows that to be alone is not to be lonely. Then silence will adorn the journey of looking within from a new promise of humility. To await and encounter the King of kings is, therefore, a long preparation in the blessings of silence :

> Under the great sky in solitude and silence, with humble heart shall I stand before thee face to face.
>
> In this laborious world of thine, tumultuous with toil and with struggle, among hurrying crowds shall I stand before thee face to face.
>
> And when my work shall be done in this world, O King of kings, alone and speechless shall I stand before thee face to face.[13]

The recognise the King of kings is to recognise the silence that crowns the earth. Tagore makes a significant identification of the mystic appearance of the King who embodies within Himself both the sky and the nest. The morning with her golden basket or the evening with the language of loneliness are all marks of mystic beauty where white radiance *sans* colour *sans* form *sans* day and night *sans* any word speaks about the sky that endlessly beckons the soul. To entertain the King with such a mystic purity of vision with words of invocation is a serene task which can be performed by a mystic visionary alone. As Tagore exposes,

> Thou art the sky and thou art the nest as well.
>
> O thou beautiful, there in the nest it is thy love that encloses the soul with colours and sounds and odours.
>
> There comes the morning with the golden basket in her right hand bearing the wreath of beauty, silently to crown the earth.
>
> And there comes the evening over the lonely meadows deserved by herds, through trackless paths, carrying cool draughts of peace in her golden pitcher from the western ocean of rest.
>
> But there, where spreads the infinite sky for the soul to take her flight in, reigns the stainless white radiance. There is no day nor night, nor form nor colour, and never, never a word.[14]

The mingling of day and night, form and colour is the poised vision of fulness—the vision that one encapsulates within oneself from the depth of mystic poignance. In such poignance of vision the child in one is in full creativity. The play is endless—the play that goes on unhindered. The hidden treasures of life have no attraction nor is there any interest in the petty affairs of life. Life, on the other hand, is enkindled with the spirit of total dedication, total submission to the Creator Eternal. A fusion of the mind of the child with that of Child Eternal can alone make a picturesque presentation as follows :

> They build their houses with sand and they play with empty shells. With withered leaves they weave their boats and smilingly float them on the vast deep. Children have their play on the seashore of worlds.

> They know not how to swim, they know not how to cast nets, Pearl fishers dive for pearls, merchants sail in their ships, while children gather pebbles and scatter them again. They seek not for hidden treasures, they know not how to cast nets.[15]

The concept of the child in all its mystic efflorescence appeals to Tagore more than anything else. In the child he finds the seeds of both life and death. In it, too, he finds the mystic vision of life and death-fondled and nourished by the mother's breast. The morning of life with all its mystery of pulsating moments finds a new vision of poignance and beyonding of consciousness, when the formless appears before him in the form of a mother. No strangeness is there with him nor even the thought of alienation that apparently crops up with the change of morning and night, light and darkness, buoyant moment and moment of silence. Death, therefore, is a familiar figure, one's very own, who encounters not as horrible but most endearing and 'ever known' as Tagore like a serene mystic feels within himself. His mystic wonder gushes forth like a fountain in muse :

> I was not aware of the moment when I first crossed the threshold of this life.
>
> What was the power that made me open out into this vast mystery like a bud in the forest at midnight !
>
> When in the morning I looked upon the light I felt in a moment that I was no stranger in this world, that the inscrutable without name and form had taken me in its arms in the form of my own mother.
>
> Even so, in death the same unknown will appear as even known to me. And because I love this life, I know I shall love death as well.
>
> The child cries out when from the right breast the mother takes it away, in the very next moment to find in the left one its consolation.[16]

A sense of profoundness serves as an antidote to all askances all matters unexplained. Where is the last answer correct and complete from every point of view ? The scorns and the smiles of worldly life await a mystic response from the All Seer, the Omnipotent and the Omniscient. The mystic smile from Him either in association or in dissociation is the ever widening arena of wonder which prepares the mind for humble submission as the Poet does by means of his mystic muse :

> I boasted among men that I had known you. They see your pictures in all works of mine. They come and ask me, 'Who is he ?' I know not how to answer them. I say, 'Indeed, I cannot tell.' They blame me and they do away in scorn. And you sit there smiling.
>
> I put my tales of you into lasting songs. The secret gushes out from my heart. They come and ask me, 'Tell me all your meanings.' I know not how to answer them. I say, 'Ah, who knows what they mean !' They smile and go away in utter scorn. And you sit there smiling.[17]

With intimacy grown through fusion of mystic vision the Poet makes on endearing relationship between the All Serene and himself. The amazement that propels within his mind in all wonder amidst silence takes the form of adoration and wistfulness. He longs to be mingled in the holy stream of music of that Great Musician whose lore crosses over all constraints like the surging waves undaunted by any obstacle whatsoever and rush on in full freedom.The deep enchantment of music that the All Serene produces through His song makes him a captive. The moment of mystic appreciation is arrested in the moment of silence and wonder. The inward cry remains unheard. The failure of being nearer to the All Serene is not altogether a failure. For the lore of the baffled heart readily exposes the inward mystic vision in silent amazement :

> The light of thy music illumines the world.
> The life breath of thy music runs from sky to sky.

> The holy stream of thy music breaks through all stony obstacles and rushes on.
>
> My heart longs to join in thy song, but vainly struggles for a voice. I would speak, but speech breaks not into song, and I cry out baffled. Ah, thou hast made my heart captive in the endless meshes of thy music, my master.[18]

Is the master a mystic baffler or is He the eternal fountain of inspiration ? A mesmeric mystic poet admits all indulgence allowed by the master. The Great Spirit tears him apart for the failure to be won over in fulness of mystic vision. But how ? Should he remain isolated in silence caged and cornered by defeat in the room of loneliness ? No. He wants to be a partner to the master through 'endless toil in a shoreless sea of toil'. The summer of a sea of activities all around in the exquisite beauty of Nature brings forth a new perfume of promise. He cannot allow the moment of moments to be left uncared for and unutilized. It is the supreme moment of dedication of life—the moment when there is the rare opportunity to be a partner to the All Serene in mystic fulfilment :

> Away from the sight of thy face my heart knows no rest nor respite, and my work becomes an endless toil in a shoreless sea of toil.
>
> Today the summer has come at my window with its sight and murmurs; and the bees are plying their minstrelsy at the court of the flowering grove.
>
> Now it is time to sit quiet, face to face with thee, and to sing dedication of life in this silent overflowing leisure.[19]

Elsewhere, the poet expresses the same objective explained in terms of fulfilment of 'the happy moment' when the All Beautiful will be encountered. To wait and to watch in delight is to wait and to watch for the moment of that happy encounter. Meanwhile, it is time to be prepared through smile and music. The blessed loneliness makes room for such a preparation. The 'perfume of promise' is there all around in the mystic aura of brilliance in Nature, and so the Poet smiles and sings in delight :

> This is my delight, thus to wait and watch at the wayside where shadow chases light and the rain comes in the wake of the summer.
>
> Messengers, with tidings from unknown skies, greet me and speed along the road. My heart is glad within, and the breath of the passing breeze is sweet.
>
> From dawn till dusk I sit here before my door, and I know that of a sudden the happy moment will arrive when I shall see.
>
> In the meanwhile I smile and I sing all alone. In the meanwhile the air is filling with the perfume of promise.[20]

The mystic imagery of the All Serene, the Master and the poet, a prisoner at the hands of the Master is simply incomparable and superb. A dramatic poignance sets the whole imagery agog with finer sense of vision and deeper involvement with the Master. The initial set is well portrayed in the canvas of conscience restored and recrystallized with the companionship of the Master, a bed-fellow who leaves him to be reawakened in the morning as a prisoner in the abandoned treasure-house.

The final set is of greater mystic poignance. The futile glory of 'invincible power', and an unusual longing for vain freedom are set against captivity in work in abstraction. The Master, the eternal chain breaker as the poet mystically visualizes, leaves the note in the end that all work is a humble submission to the Great Master. Here is the wonderful mystic muse that runs like a dramatic monologue of the most vibrant inward vision of life common to mankind :

> 'Prisoner, tell me, who was it that bound you ?'
>
> 'It was my master', said the prisoner. 'I thought I could outdo everybody in the world in health and power, and I amassed in my own treasure-house the money due to my king. When sleep overcame me I lay upon the bed that was for my Lord, and my own treasure-house.'
>
> 'Prisoner, tell me, who was it that wrought this unbreakable chain ?'
>
> 'It was I', said the prisoner, 'who forged this chain very carefully. I thought my invincible power would hold the world captive leaving me in a freedom undisturbed. Thus night and day I worked at the chain with huge fires and cruel hard strokes. When at last the work was done and the links were complete and unbreakable, I found that it held me in its grip.'[21]

The fetter of the love of God as the poet visualizes in mystic poignance is the one that prompts him to offer his love at every moment. To 'surrender my strength' as he wishes and prays ardently 'to thy will with love' in his address to the All Serene makes his voyage unending in mystic transcendence from beauty to serenity, from pomp to simplicity and from boisterousness and vitality to calmness and humble submission. The storm that goes on in his mind seeks an end in peace by welcoming the King of kings in the halo of mystic effulgence.

Meanwhile, the ecstasy of mystic fulfilment bursts forth in the inward wailing : 'I want thee, only thee.'

Why not each of us be a partner to the poet's mystic vision in the inward wailing as above ?

REFERENCES

1. Tagore, Rabindranath : Gitanjali, Macmillan India Limited, New Delhi, Macmillan Pocket Tagore Edition, 1983. No. XIX, p. 11-12.

2. *Ibid*. No. XXV, p.15

3. *Ibid*. No. III, p.2-3

4. *Ibid*. No. V, p. 3-4

5. *Ibid*. No. XXVI, p. 15

6. *Ibid*. No. XIV, p. 9

7. *Ibid*. No. LIII p. 34-35

8. Sri Aurobindo : "Rose of God", Transformation and other Poems, Sri Aurobindo Ashram, Pondicherry.

9. Tagore, Rabindranath : *Gitanjali*, Macmillan India Limited, New Delhi, Macmillan Pocket Tagore Edition, 1983, No. LX., p. 39.

10. *Ibid*. No. XXVII, p. 15-16

11. *Ibid*. No. XXXIX, p. 22-23

12. *Ibid*. No. XLI, p. 24-25

13. *Ibid*. No. LXXVI, p. 51

14. *Ibid*. No. LXVII, p. 41

15. *Ibid*. No. LX, p. 39

16. *Ibid*. No. XCV, p. 62-63

17. *Ibid*. No. CII, p. 67

18. *Ibid*.No. III, p. 2-3

19. *Ibid*. No. V, p. 4

20. *Ibid*. No. XLIV, p. 26

21. *Ibid*. No. XXXI, p. 18

THE CONCEPT OF TRANSCENDENCE IN TAGORE'S FOLK SONGS

The world of folk songs is the world of the inner man, the man within man. It is the man in his best essence, best excellence in exposition not seen but felt, not understood but appreciated with utmost sincerity and devotion. For Tagore, the world of folk songs is the world of transcendence of man. It is the world that takes man nearer to the man of the Heart for whom man haunts and haunts eternally to have a glimpse of Him for once and for once only. Why does man do so ? Is the yearning for the man of the Heart—*maner manush*—a yearning for the beyonding of consciousness ? Is it a longing most poignant and serene ? Certainly so. Otherwise, where is the light, the Great Awakener of the inner man ? Tagore is very explicit when he clarifies the nature of a homeless wanderer—a *baul*— in unending search for the mystic and transcendental poignance of man :

> 'The man of the Heart', to the Baul, is like a divine instrument perfectly tuned. He gives expression to infinite truth in the music of life. And the longing for the truth which is in us, which we have not yet realized breaks out in the following Baul song :

Where shall I meet him, the Man of my Heart ?
He is lost to me and I seek him wandering from land
to land,
I am listless for that moonrise of beauty,
Which is to light my life,
Which I long to see in the fulness of vision, in
gladness of heart.[1]

The search for the Man of the Heart is, indeed, frantic and ceaseless. The askance is not apparent but within the mind. The stars at night in darkness in the eternal silence of wonder make the moment of transcendence sacred in sincere preparation of the mind. The sea, the southern wind, and the bright glowing sunlight are all agog with the moment when the unknown person plays on the flute to herald the auspicious encounter with the All Beautiful. The poignance of transcendence finds a new language of emotion when the Poet goes on musing in words that sound like a serene soliloquy :

Mind, O Mind, of what meditation you are the
outcome
I find you not, only seeking all the time
The stars close not their eyes—seeking in darkness
The southern wind calls on you everywhere
As the sea raises sound and seeks its own gem
So the sunlight shines all over the sky
Who is the unknown person that calls you by
the name and plays on the flute ?[2]

Deeply influenced by the spirit of transcendence in the *baul* songs of Bengal, Tagore appreciates the beauty of simplicity and earnestness of the heart expressed in these songs that want to make an intense bond of synchronization with the universe. A new world of consciousness with which any one becomes familiar whenever these songs of transcendence are sung makes him more devoted to enter deep into the world of the inner muse of re-awakening. In fact, the impression that he received about the transcendental elements of the folk songs of Bengal has been clearly expressed in one of his letters as follows :

Those who have read my writings know that I have expressed my devotion to *Baul Padavalis* in many of my writings. When I was at Shelaidah, I always met and talked with the group of bauls. In many of my songs, I have accepted the tunes of the bauls, and in many songs the union of the baul tunes with the other tune-patterns with or without my knowledge. From this, it may be understood that the tunes and words of the bauls have at a certain period, easily mingled with me. I remember, in the very Shelaidah area, a baul sang with an *ektara* (a single string musical instrument of the bauls) :

> *Kothay pavo tare*
> *Amar maner manush je re.*
> (Where shall I find Him,
> The Man of my mind.)

The words are very simple, but their meaning brightened with a unique lustre in association with tuning. I heard from the non-scholar in his rustic tune and in simple language—the pain of not knowing Him least, whom one should know most, has been tuned in his voice "*Antaratara yadayamatma* ("This soul is more endearing"). When I heard this message of the Upanishad from their voice as *Maner Manush* ("Man of the Mind"), I was greatly astonished. I have heard such a baul's song as is incomparable in respect of simplicity of language, intensity of ideas and in empathy of tune. Just as it is in unison with the theories of knowledge, so is the composition of poetry coupled with the poignance of *Bhakti* (devotion). I do not believe there is any such brilliance anywhere as available in folk literature.[3]

To switch over from the self to the Supreme Being, from personal to the impersonal All Serene and yet maintain a harmonious relationship in love and hope, joy and sorrow are the strategic avenues of transcendence that Tagore chooses to tread on. He loses himself in joy in rustic simplicity that itself represents one of the most potent qualities to be in unison with the All Simple and Serene. The encounter becomes one with the self and the Divine Self—the encounter for which a truly homeless minstrel goes on singing unendingly. As an incomparable inward visionary, Tagore also seeks within the All Endearing hidden in the inmost core of his heart. As he muses on,

> You remained hidden in my heart, I could not see
> I looked wide outside, towards my heart I looked not,
> In all my love, in all strokes and hopes
> You were beside me, I went not nearby you
> Like my joy you remained in my play
> So I lost myself in joy, the days idly spent
> In the poignant heart in secret, in my songs of joy and sorrow
> You have given tunes but I did not sing your songs.[4]

How is Tagore baptised in the spirit of transcendence in his folk songs ? Where does he find out the fountain of inspiration ? It is Jnandas, his favourite folk singer, whom he considers in his heart of hearts to be the true exponent of transcendental love and devotion to the All Loving. As a matter of fact, he finds great delight and moving inspiration in translating the songs of Jnandas. Here is an example rich in the philosophy of transcendence of love :

> I had travelled all day and was tired; then I bowed my head towards thy kingly court still far away
> The night deepened, a longing burned in my heart.
> Whatever the words I sang, pain cried through them—for even my songs thirsted...
> O my Lover, my Beloved, my Best in all the world.

When time seemed lost in darkness, thy hand
dropped in sceptre to take up the
lute and strike the uttermost chords;
And my heart sang out,
O my Lover, my Beloved, my Best in all the
world.

Ah, who is this whose arms enfold me ?
'Whatever I have to leave, let me leave; and
whenever I have to bear, let me bear.
Only let me walk with thee,
O my Lover, my Beloved, my Best in all the
world.

Descend at whiles from thy high audience hall,
come down amid joys and sorrows.
Hide in all forms and delights, in love,
And in my heart sing thy songs...
O my Lover, my Beloved, my Best in all the
world.[5]

How does Tagore initiate himself with the 'Best in all the world' ? Leaving aside 'the inaccessible mountain peaks of theology' he finds the resonance of the religion of transcendence in the simple, unambiguous, plain, rustic folk songs which truly reveals the spirit of man the Divine. His own words in this connection are the outcome of his deep personal experience in association with the exponents of folk songs from introspective points of view :

> It is needless to say...that I had neither the training nor the opportunity to study this mendicant religious sect in Bengal from an ethnological standpoint. I was attracted to find out how the living currents of religious movements work in the heart of the people, saving them from degradation imposed by the society of the learned, of the rich, or of the high-born; how the spirit of man, by making use even of its obstacles, reaches fulfilment, led thither, not by the learned

> authorities in the scriptures, or by the mechanical impulse of the dogma-driven crowd, but by the unsophisticated aspiration of the loving soul. On the inaccessible mountain peaks of theology the snows of creed remain eternally rigid, cold, and pure. But God's manifest shower falls direct on the plain of humble hearts, flowing there in various channels, even getting mixed with some mud in its course, as it is soaked into the underground currents, invisible, but ever-moving.[6]

So ardent is Tagore to be in unison with the 'humble hearts' that he yearns for encounter with the All Simple as represented by ones who cultivate or play on the flute. The inward transcendence allows him to have the bird as his companion, partner and informer of the great news that the Lord of the heart is always playing with all mysteries not anywhere else but within himself. Here is the yearning expressed in exquisite words of sincere lore :

> Unite me with them who tend your cows,
> who play on the flute in your name.
> On the stone-built bank, in this meleé of chaos,
> why and for what attraction did I come.
> What's the call of the forest leaves whose
> beckonings are thro' the grass
> The God of my heart does play in the playhouse of
> the heart with all mysteries,
> This is the news that from the mouth of birds did I
> receive.[7]

To make a happy comradeship with Nature the great sustainer is to be on the right track of transcendence. When Tagore treads on such a track with the full-throated voice of the simple folk, he finds a great deal of intoxicating aroma of involvement with the All Beautiful. The haunting spirit of the poet-singer finds an altogether different canvas of transfusion. The eluding spirit of the Great Intoxicator beckons him to join the chorus of creative transcendence.

The vision of the All Beautiful everywhere is the vision of transcendence. It is the vision that promotes a serene marriage of minds between the poet-singer and the creator. Is such a transcendence a re-birth of man ? Perhaps so. For Tagore, it is the great occasion to visualize and to be in unison with the All Serene within the light and the stars that glow in one's own vision. What a revelation in the lore of transcendence ! Here is the poet-singer's frank confession :

> I seek Him alone who lives in my mind.
> As He does exist,
> Stars shine in the sky of my mind at night
> Flowers bloom in my forest in the morning.
> As He does exist,
> In the light of the stars of the eyes
> There's so much of play of beauty and feast of colour in endless black and white.
> As he remains with me,
> The southern wind awakens my joy in my every limb,
> His message it is that is filled
> In the tune of my song amid an unmindful *taan*
> He swings me in the sweep of sorrow all on a sudden
> He conceals Himself amidst work and makes me forget my work.
> As eternal He is to me
> It is His gladness that at times filled in my moments.[8]

The transcendence that speaks of transfer of mind between the Creator and His singer is all evident in the song of simplicity. Like a simple unassuming *baul,* Tagore brings forth the rhythm of intoxicating music that floats on with the unending muse of the flute. The play goes on—the play of hide and seek with the All Beautiful and the inherent aroma of transcendence pours forth with the vibrant tune as he sings in eternal askance :

Who is that intoxicator that goes on haunting me
from one locality to the other.
O, what a lovely tuning is there all over the sky in
the wind unknown !
The day dies down. What a game of the
intoxicator !
He spells a web in His call but remains away.
I seek Him in forests and mountains, in what an
agony do I go on crying ![9]

The liberation that Tagore seeks through his folk songs is one that has its transcendence in the midst of love. Love, to him, is a unifying force that make a serene cohesion between him and the All Beautiful. He, therefore, seeks the sky of his heart in the sky of the Man of the heart—*maner manush*. As he muses,

I know in thy love the message of all love mingles
I seek my salvation in it alone at the day's end,
The greatest meditation of love is there, all its
bonds are loosened
In thy heart is the sky of the bird of my heart.
O Dear, know I that all the streams of my tired
days
Become tireless in the bliss of thy dense-deep night
The touch of the earth in my body has become
lively with thy drink
The very wealth of my dust adores within Thee in
a new pattern.[10]

The humble submission that Tagore makes to the All Serene is a way of transcendence that he chooses to liberate himself from darkness and ignorance, emptiness and desolation. Forlorn as he is in the world of inconsistencies and imperfections he badly seeks comradeship with the All Beautiful who would come nearer to his heart and speak His message of emancipation. He feels in his heart of hearts that the only way to eliminate the filth and dirt of his mind is to transcend himself to the All Beautiful. Here is his muse resonant with the spirit of humble dedication :

Please accept me now, O my Lord, accept me
O, please do not refuse me now.
Remain seizing my heart.

I do not want again the day lost *sans* you.
Let it go to dust.

Now let me allow to remain awake day and night
By expanding my life in your light

With what an aroma and in what a word
Have I roamed everywhere
In cities and in fields !

Tell me now the message of your own
Hiding your face nearer my heart.

So many stains and so many truancies
Are yet remained in the depth of the mind

Please do not tell me to go back once more for these,
Burn these with fire.[11]

The journey from pleasure to pain is a journey of serene transcendence. In his folk songs, Tagore paves this path of transcendence with adroit imageries. He submits himself whole-heartedly to the All Beloved. He never wants to depart from the latter. Pleasure and pain are both ornamented in the hallowed touch of love of the All Beloved. And so is the eternal joy for him in the transcendence of love :

Thou hast made me weep with the stroke of thy love.
In intense pain I feel joy in me.
I shall go to the shores of the unreachable in search of thee.
Let pain tune on during my journey on every avenue.
The beauty of sorrow made me lose direction.
Thou wouldst snatch away all, yet wouldst thou leave nothing.

The mind does not desire to depart, O in what a
mess hast thou bound me ![12]

The essence of transcendence as Tagore hints at through his folk songs is to be found in his concept of freedom of the man of the heart, the man *par excellence.* To nursle this concept of freedom is to nursle the spirit of transcendence which lead man to be in unison with the All Beautiful. As this sort of unison is beyond time and circumstances, it is the duty of every one to adore and honour the All Beautiful by denying pain and sorrow, night and darkness, languishment and separation. As the All Beautiful is beyond all bonds of attraction, it is better that one should highlight the spirit of transcendence in the warmth of freedom. In the Tagorean words of muse,

The Man of the Heart He is, why do you keep Him
seated beside the door of your eyes;
Why not call Him in your breast, let eyes be
washed away with the streams of eyes !
When lights will be extinguished and the night
will come, spread the seat in your heart.
In darkness of separation will He in secret arrive.
In His secret path of arrival and departure
In His own accord will He come and depart.
When you promise to bind Him, He remains not, the
string does remain.
Bind yourself aside with that string alone.[13]

A sense of gratitude that emanates from the above is the *sine qua non* of the spirit of transcendence that the poet heralds all through his creative activities. There is also a certain sense of numbness in his muse that appeals to the inner core of the heart. This concept of transcendence in his folk songs has its adherence to some of the immortal songs that we come across in *Gitanjali* (*Song Offerings*). Here, for example, is how he exposes the spirit of transcendence in the form of dedication to the All Beautiful :

Thy gifts to us mortals fulfil all our needs
and yet run back to thee undiminished.

The river has its everyday work to do
and hastens through fields and hamlets;
yet its incessant stream winds towards
the washing of thy feet.

The flower sweetens the air with its perfume;
yet its last service is to offer itself to thee.

Thy worship does not impoverish the world.
From the words of the poet men take
What meanings please them; yet their last
meaning points to thee.[14]

To be a total loser at the hands of the All Beautiful is, as Tagore believes, to be an endless gainer, for fulness in oneself depends on how one empties oneself for better transcendence. How does Tagore remain true to this theory of transcendence ? Let us listen to the muse that reveals his transcendental vision :

When I was bereft of vision
My time was spent in the play of tunes but I found no joy.
Building the walls of the playhouse, I was rapt in whims
When you came by cracking the foundation, my bondage is over
The game of happiness I like no more, I have found joy.
O my Terrible, my Fierce, my little slumber is gone
You've tuned up my rhythm with violent pains anew
The day when in the guise of fire you took away my all
I became perfect on that day and my conflicts came to an end.
O joy, I have been in unison with you beyond the banks of sorrow and happiness.[15]

The avenues of the concept of transcendence as Tagore opens by means of his folk songs are diverse and multi-dimensional where man merges in the millennium of joy and sorrow, hopes and failures, laughter and tears to usher forth the spirit of fusion in transcendence. When shall we follow his footpoints in the full-throated folk songs of fulness ?

REFERENCES

1. Rabindranath Tagore : "An Indian Folk Religion", *Creative Unity,* Macmillan & Co. Ltd., London, 1962, p. 78-79.

2. Rabindranath Tagore : *Songs, Rabindra-Rachanavali,* Government of West Bengal, Calcutta, 1980, Vol. IV, No. 1613, p. 614.

   Translated by the author.

3. Santidev Ghose : *"Rabindranath O Banglar Baul"* ("Rabindranath and the Bauls of Bengal"), *Rabindrasangeet Vichitra* ("Rabindrasangeet Miscellany"). Ananda Publishers Private Limited, Calcutta, 1987, p. 98. Translated by the author.

4. Rabindranath Tagore : *Songs, Rabindra-Rachanavali,* Government of West Bengal, Calcutta, 1980, Vol. IV, No. 905, p. 375. Translated by the author.

5. Rabindranath Tagore : "An Indian Folk Religion, "*Creative Unity,* Macmillan & Co. Ltd., London., 1962, p. 89-90.

6. *Ibid*. p. 88-89

7. Rabindranath Tagore : *Songs, Rabindra-Rachanavali,* Government of West Bengal, Calcutta, 1980, Vol. IV, No. 900, p. 373. Translated by the author.
8. *Ibid.* No. 1097. p. 443. Translated by the author.
9. *Ibid.* No. 673. p. 292. Translated by the author.
10. *Ibid.* No. 1528. p. 585. Translated by the author.
11. *Ibid.* No. 733. p. 312. Translated by the author.
12. *Ibid.* No. 1554. p. 595. Translated by the author.
13. *Ibid.* No. 1392. p. 538. Translated by the author.
14. Rabindranath Tagore : *Gitanjali (Song Offerings),* Macmillan India Limited, Macmillan Pocket Tagore Edition, 1983, No. LXXV, p. 50.
15. Rabindranath Tagore : *Songs, Rabindra-Rachanavali,* Government of West Bengal, Calcutta, 1980, Vol. IV, No. 1614, p. 615. Translated by the author.

FAREWELL TO EARTH : TAGORE'S VISION OF DEATH

Death, to Rabindranath Tagore, is a beyonding of consciousness. It is a vision of the All Beautiful–endless and serene, poignant and elegant, calm and majestic. The parting between the lover and the beloved, the living and the dead is a symbol of unison inseparable and eternal somewhere beyond the horizon of life and death. As a foreseer of the beyonding of life and death, Tagore spells out his inner vision in terms of unending poignance of music :

Leaving the realms of life and death
Thou hast remained standing, O my friend !
In this lonely sky of the heart of mine
Thy great seat is covered with light
With what a poignant hope and intense joy
I look at that, stretching my two arms
The silent night has spread o'er thy feet
The burden of hair of darkness.
What a song has o'erflooded the world
And has come down from your *Veena* !
The earth is in unison with the resonants of tunes
And I lose myself in the pain of songs.
[*'Jivan Maraner Simana Chhadaya'* : Pooja : Translated by the Author.]

Deeply distressed and wounded by loss of near and dear ones including children and wife, Tagore stands against death in rocklike firmness *sans* desolation *sans* hopelessness. What armour does he prescribe against all oddities of life ? It is joy and joy alone. It is joy that brings forth eternal nectar (*chira-amrita*) and translates all experiences into an offering for the All True, All Good, All Beautiful. Here is his unparalleled prescription :

> Remain in joy all the time in the world fearless and
> with a heart pure
> Awake in joy in the morning, work in joy,
> In songs of joy return home in the evening.
> Remain in goodness in crisis and affluence,
> In disgrace and dishonour remain in joy,
> In joy remain by pardoning all,
> In drinking peace in the fountain of nectar for ever.
>
> [*'Sada thako anande'* : *Pooja* : Translated by the Author.]

A visionary *par excellence* as he is, Tagore prepares himself for the last journey by correlating himself with the halo of the Eternal. The Kingdom of endless joy beckons him with the promise of eternal gifts of Truth that make life meaningful. The mystery of disappointment awaits a fitting farewell and so he prays for peace and silence at such a hallowed and auspicious moment for the Great Meeting :

> Oft do I think as if the time for adieu has come
> Cast the veil on the day of farewell
> Of the light of the controlled setting sun
> Let the parting time
> Be peaceful and silent, let not the assembly of
> condolence
> Create the illusion of bereavement.
>
> [*Arogya:* Poem No. 31. Translated by the Author.]

The grand assembly of the seven saints of heaven cannot be missed. The poet has introspectively visualized peace coming down to earth with the silent blessings that the night brings forth for the parting moments :

> Let the rows of forest at the door of departure
> Proclaim the message of peace of the world with the assembly of leaves
> Let the silent blessings of the night—
> The offerings of the halo of seven saints—
> Come down.
>
> [*Ibid.* Translated by the Author.]

Farewell to earth does not bring forth defeat to the poet. Rather is he grateful to the Creator of the earth for the honour he has received, and so the imminent hours of farewell make him evaluate the present in terms of the past. The sense of desolation leads him to a confession frank but down to earth :

> Day after day wanes away, silently I remain seated
>
> Thinking over the gifts of life how much is left
> By meeting the wastage of savings.
> What is waned *sans* care,
> Whate'er due I have received, whate'er to be given I've delivered
> What is left as the remnant for the end.
> Those who came near, those who went far away
> With what tuning of mine their touch has still remained
> Whom I recognized not in absentmindedness !
> The footfalls of farewell to-day are ringing in the heart in vain
> Perhaps I knew not who had left away forgiving me
> Without speaking.
>
> [*Arogya* : Poem No. 16. Translated by the Author.]

Being aware of his own limitations as a living being, the poet begs farewell to earth through apologies of one and all. Let the ardent bonds of relationship between him and others be strengthened with the warm welcome of Beauty and the invitation of the young vibrant with pulsating moments of life with the blooming redness of *palash*.

The halo of consciousness luminous in the firmament of his mind thrusts the poet face to face with a categorical assertion : everything wanes with farewell to earth, but an exception still remains. It is one's creation which lasts even after death. For death is a passport to understand and appreciate the new in lieu of the old which turns out to be new again with the aroma of creativity and love and affection for the earth. Here is a grateful confession by the poet :

> I do not have faith in my achievements
> Know I that the sea of time
> With strokes of waves all the time
> Would wipe it away day by day.
>
> Myself do I believe
> Filling that cup day and night
> The eternal juice of this universe
> Have I drunk.
>
> The love of every moment
> Amid it has been stored
> The burden of sorrow tattered it not
> Nor dust blackened
> Its artistry.
>
> Know I that when I would bid farewell
> To the battle stage of the world
> The forest of flowers would at every season give
> evidence
> That I have loved this universe.
>
> This love alone is truth—a gift of this life.
> At the time of bidding farewell
> This truth untarnished would defy death.
>
> [*Rogashajyay:* Poem No. 26, p. 805. Translated by
> the Author.]

The sense of gratefulness that the poet bears within throughout his life finds a greater intensity of efflorescence at the time of farewell to earth. With the waning of days like flowers from the flower vase of his life, death for him is an awakening afresh. It is a unison between life and death with an exchange of vision in a glorious dramatic denouement serene and calm in words of gratitude :

The mind says, farewell.
My salute do I leave behind
For those who have on the path of life
Flashed light that has erased out fear again and again.

[*Janmadine* : Poem No. 12. Translated by the Author.]

Farewell to earth is welcome to earth again, and this belief has strengthened the poet to welcome death wholeheartedly. The pain of death promises the pleasure of a happy return. As the poet muses,

If you save me not, why do you kill me ?
Why this preparation amidst such a clamour ?
The arrow-case is filled with firesome arrows, the earth trembles under feet.
The deliverer of life is agog with the feast of death
What would happen to the breast you tear off in such a way if no fountain springs off ?
This mine of pain within me would provide that gem of your crown.
The partner of my life shall I awake with the sufferings of death.

[*Na vachave amay yadi marve keno tave : Pooja* : Translated by the Author .]

Death for the poet is a grand revelation of Truth. Farewell to the old is welcome to the new. Sorrow begets peace and joy. Life goes on with a new promise, a new beginning. Death is, therefore, never an expression of emptiness but a perennial promise of fulness. The poet's muse bears that evidence :

> Sorrow there is, death is there, the pangs of separation ache
> Yet there is peace, and joy, yet the unending awakes
> Yet life flows on and on, the sun and the moon and the stars laugh
> With variegated *raagas* does the spring appear in the garden
> Waves erase out and rise
> Flowers wither and bloom
> No decay is there nor no end nor even a bit of poverty—
> At the feet of that fulness does the mind pray to be placed.
>
> [*Aachhe dukkha, aachhe mrityu, virahadahana lage* : *Pooja* : Translated by the Author.]

For a true comradeship with death, the poet wants to wipe off all barriers. Let the meeting between Death and him be as endearing and joyful as he ardently desires. At the time of bidding farewell to death, he, therefore, heartily welcomes Death to take him away to the land of eternal joy :

> Stealthily do thou comest in the dark night
> Thou art my friend
> And clasp me in strong hands
> Thou art my joy.
> Thou art the lone charioteer of the chariot of sorrow
> Thou art my friend alone.
> Thou art the crisis, loss thou art,
> Thou art my joy.
> An enemy am I, win me o'er,
> Thou art my friend alone.
> Furious thou art, the fear of fears,
> Thou art my joy.

Come ye thunder, tearing off the breast,
        Thou art my friend alone.
Take ye Death, breaking off the barriers,
        Thou art my joy.

[*Lukie aaso andhar rate, tumi amar vandhu* : *Pooja* : Translated by the Author.]

A foreseer of the end or the beginning of life anew, the poet highlights death as the greatest moment of unison with Light. His farewell to earth is marked with a halo of consciousness that brings forth for him that light of joy of the Man Eternal. The moment of farewell to the earth is one of a great revelation of experiences of life translated in words of prayer :

Let the cocoon of this life unmask
The bright halo of consciousness, and
Express the Eternal form of Truth
by piercing the mist.
Let the light of joy of a Man Eternal
Amid all men
be enkindled in my mind.
Beyond the silent world of worldly grievances
Let me behold the blessed form of the Eternal.
What is amply meaningless and critical in this life,
Whatever embodies falsehood in the sham value
                                        of the society,
Leaving aside all beggarly and
Troubled crowd
Let me know the true meaning with my vivid eyes
Prior to crossing the bar.

[*Arogya* : Poem No. 33. Translated by the Author.]

Is the poet fully prepared for farewell to earth ? What will he leave behind prior to crossing the bar ? Here is the answer in his address to the Lord of Death :

Death, thy servant, is at my door. He has crossed the unknown sea and brought thy call to my home.

> The night is dark and my heart is fearful—yet I will take up the lamp, open my gates and bow to him my welcome. It is thy messenger who stands at my door.
>
> I will worship him with folded hands, and with tears. I will worship him placing at his feet the treasure of my heart.
>
> I will go back with his errand done, leaving a dark shadow on my morning; and in my desolate home only my forlorn self will remain as my last offering to thee.
>
> [*Gitanjali* : No. LXXXVI]

When comes such a visionary ?

To wait for the beautiful dawn of farewell to earth is to be assured of the ever loving guidance of the All Beautiful who remains with living conscience. As a matter of fact, the poet makes a personal relationship with the Creator on whom he safely depends and submits his heart's yearnings unhesitatingly. In such an action he easily liberates himself from his 'I' that clings to the earth and holds himself high above to be true to his second 'I' that celebrates death *sans* agonies. The life in death that Tagore discovers and celebrates is a wonderful testimony to farewell to earth. As Professor Pabitra Sarkar characteristically reveals,

> All along this prolonged interface with death, Tagore develops a very personal attitude towards it. It is romanticized, personified and allegorized in various ways, but no fear psychosis lies behind such treatments of death by the poet. He never wants to run away from it; its face to him is never ugly or fearsome. It is, on the contrary, beautiful, a fascinating *maya* perhaps. Only to ordinary mortals it has a terrifying countenance. Do not be afraid of death, Tagore assures us. A suckling child taken off from a breast of the mother cries out in

> agony, but it is soon consoled when offered the other breast. Tagore often splits himself into two selves (*'dui ami'*),—one restricted by space-time-corporeality, dogged by suffering and death, while the other, detached and ethereal, is untrammelled by these bonds, and undeterred by human agonies of death. All of Tagore's celebrations of life, therefore, can be easily translated into the celebration of death, as he looks at it, entwined with and inseparable from life.
>
> — Pabitra Sarkar : 'Life in death'—'Rabindranath Tagore : 132nd Birth Anniversary', *The Statesman,* Saturday, May 8, 1993, Supplement. P-I.

Admittedly, the moment of death for Tagore is a moment quite known and as such when his play is over in this world he believes that the All Beautiful is there who beckons him to be in unison with Him to sing the glory of His greatness as a creator and emancipator. To respond to His beckoning is to highlight death in its worthiness, and, as such, it is nothing but trekking from light to light from life to newer life. Therefore, farewell to earth is a journey to the All Beautiful who will adore his life and accept him like a flower. As he muses,

O know I that with dawn thy boat of blessings
 on the edge of the sea of the world would
 take one
Fear do I not, I would depart by singing thy victory
 And stand on thy deathless door.
O know I that stretching thy arms from age to age
 In the endless world hast thou kept me,
From light to light hast thou given me life
 from life to life hast thou transcended me.
O Lord, know I that in virtue and vice
 My heart is always at rest by thy eyes,
On my hand is thy one day and night

In all paths or *sans* path, in weal and woe.
O know I, I know that life would never be in vain,
In the sea of destruction or fear, thou wouldst
not thrust asunder
A day would come when with pity
Thou wouldst pick him up like a flower.

— Rabindranath Tagore : 'Songs', *Rabindra-Rachanavali,* Government of West Bengal, Calcutta, 1987, Vol. IV, No. 485, p. 226. [Translated by the Author.]

Is death sorrowful or is it a matter of happiness ? To Tagore, it is neither sorrow nor happiness, but it is a passport to receive poignant peace. So, when he bids farewell to earth, he is sure that the All Beautiful has come to him like a fellow traveller to lead him to the world of light.

The journey to the beyonding to have an encounter with the All Beautiful is always fascinating. To Tagore, farewell to earth is not merely fascinating but also serene because he eyes the vision of the All Beautiful before him in the form of Light Eternal. He wants to bathe in the fountain of light. He wants to be free from all worries and anxieties. Now is the time for him to be in unison with Light—Light Beautiful.

What a farewell !

TAGORE'S "CRISIS IN CIVILIZATION" : A RE-THINKING

'Civilization', as the term suffers from too much of formalism lapses in the orthodox meaning of a 'system, stage of social development'. From a broader viewpoint, it includes the philosophy of bringing humanity 'from a savage or ignorant condition to a higher one (by giving education in Methods of government, moral teaching etc.)' which in practice is tailored to the temporal needs of a particular community, society or nation and hardly caters to the diverse developments of the global society.

Quite iconoclastic in his viewpoints on civilization, Tagore finds the loopholes of the so-called civilized world of the West. The clash between humanism and radicalism often at the expense of social conscience does not avert his humane eyes. The fact that in our modern days of 'sad disillusionment'—a straight-cut Tagorean expression—we fall back upon a stereotyped line of advancement in our thought and action which neither allows us to advance nor does it allow us to retard to the good old days of finer values and greater sensibilities.

When Tagore refers to *'sadachar'* from Manu, he actually equates it to proper conduct—a quality that represents man as a civilized human being. It is the essence of humanism. It teaches man as the most disciplined of all God's creations big or small. It also teaches a man to be 'men' in the society. In fact, Tagore is perhaps aware of the invaluable words of Matthew Arnold who considers civilization to be "the element of power of conduct, of intellect and knowledge, of beauty and of social life and manners, and all needful to build up a complete human life—we have instincts responding to them all, and requiring them all, and we are perfectly civilized only when all these instincts of our nature—all these elements of our civilization have been adequately recognized and satisfied." His own boyhood has brought reactions forthwith and his own words reveal as follows :—

> In my boyhood the English-educated section of our people felt stirrings of revolt against the rigid social code—the Bengali literature of the time carries portrayals of that revolt. In place of the set code we began to accept the ideal of 'civilization' as represented by the English term and illustrated by the British character.
>
> In my own home this change, backed by reason, was warmly greeted and its effect was felt both in theory and practice. Born in such an atmosphere, and impelled by my natural bias towards literature, I saw the British occupying a pedestal of glory.
>
> That early period of my life ended in an agony of disillusionment. I started to discover more and more how those who professed the higher civilized values could cast them aside with the utmost case, whenever their national interests were at stake.
>
> The moment came when I had to pull myself away from preoccupation with literature. For the sight of the terrible poverty of the Indian masses grew inescapable. I realized that perhaps in no other modern state was there such a complete denial of the basic needs of living : food and

> clothing, education and health services. And yet it was the exploited resources of this country that had been adding, year on year, to the wealth of the British race.
>
> Lost in the glamorous aspects of British culture, I had never thought that, out of it could come so cruel a distortion of long cherished values; that distortion, I knew at last, was the emblem of a civilized nation's contempt and callousness towards our vast masses.
>
> — Rabindranath Tagore : "Crisis in Civilization", *Towards Universal Man*, Asia Publishing House, Bombay, 1961, p. 354-355.

Interestingly enough, Tagore spearheads the attack not upon a particular nation but upon the maimed civilization which has eaten up the having, loving and being of mankind. His own experiences are so introspectively poignant that even the modern intelligentsia cannot evaluate him more in terms of a crusader in the crisis of our doled out civilization than in those of his literacy excellences and talents in performing arts ! A sentimental bias towards culture-euphoria at the threshold of the twenty-first century has also gripped Tagoreana so much so that civilization with its roots down to the depths of reality and humanism has been, more often than not, camouflaged. Even professionalism in the dissemination of Tagorean culture has allowed mushroom growth of cultism. In fact, *mohantas* make a hey day in the whirlwind of showmanship in Tagorean culture. That the truth of civilization dies in such an irony of ritualistic ecstasies needs no elucidation. Only a limited few scholars and exponents of Tagore's prophetic vision hold up the serene torch of his vision of the Universal Brotherhood of Mankind.

How to re-think Tagore in terms of his above vision of the Universal Brotherhood of Mankind ? His own suggestions would show us the exact way. True civilization is always in kissing terms with sympathy. The education of sympathy is yet a far cry. Super-computerized education laughs at the terrible massacre of civilization in Afghanistan or Bosnia. The education of sympathy still awaits a passport to enter into the heartland of humanity. That 'apathy and ignorance are the worst forms of bondage for man' so characteristically voiced by Tagore still serves as a warning signal for restoration of civilization.

More than a mere treatise on unfolding the crisis of civilization, Tagore refers in this epoch-making testament, read in his presence on the occasion of his eightieth birthday, April 14, 1941, at Santiniketan, to the dwindling condition of the-then India reeling under illiteracy, penury, disease, and all other extrinsic marks of shame in the name of civilization. What shocks him more is the unlimited racial prejudice that even now crops up in the shadow of apathy and ignorance. A country lying 'effortless and inert' under 'the immense deadweight of British rule' which has been somehow or other allowed to thrive or pauperised with vested interests can only enjoy real freedom if projection of 'the power of human fellowship' becomes a living reality. The experiences that he achieved from the dynamism of living and sharing of conjoint co-operative ideas and experiences from countries like Russia, Iran, Japan and Afghanistan are the only way-out to negotiate the wretched state of humanism.

The spirit of violence as wrongly considered to be the only answer to negotiate violence may tempt sentimental revolutionaries to bring about a radical change in stark misery but Tagore never thinks so, nor does he ever allow violence to dechannelize the spirit of goodness and human fellowship. Violence only breeds violence and kills the finer sensibilities and the softer visions of mankind.

The message to humanity as revealed in this treatise by Tagore on completing his eighty years, has its ample and rich background. Already, the experiences of eighteen months in

London during his first visit in September 1878 have served a solid background for him to nursle the seeds of Universal Brotherhood of Mankind. Added to this, are his profuse experiences received from his three-time visit to Japan in 1916, 1924 and 1929 followed by a fortnight's visit to Russia, September 11-25, 1930 and thereafter to Iran in 1922 at the invitation of Reja Shah Pahlavi, which prompt him with a promise of poignance to bring about a change in the 'poverty-shamed hovel which is India' and restore and effulge the truest spirit of humanism.

To win back the 'lost heritage' as Tagore reminds with a serene voice, with the end of cataclysm is not enough. Much is to be done to avert the crisis of crisis—the crisis that looms large in the horizon of marooned humanity. In a prophetic voice he refers to the wheel of fortune :

> The turning of the wheel of fortune will compel the British one day to give up their Indian empire. But what kind of India will they leave behind, what stark misery ? When the stream of their two countries' rule runs dry at last, what a waste of mud and filth will be revealed, bearing a tale of utter futility ! There was a time when I used to believe that the springs of a true civilization would issue out of the heart of Europe. Today, as I am about to quit the world, that faith has gone bankrupt.
>
> I live today in the hope that the Saviour is coming, that he will be born in our midst in this poverty-shamed hovel which is India. I shall wait to hear the message he brings with him, the supreme word of promise he speaks unto man from this eastern horizon to give faith and strength to all who hear.
>
> I look back on the stretch of past years and see the crumbling ruins of a proud civilization lying heaped as garbage out of history ! And yet I shall

> not commit the grievous sin of losing faith in Man, accepting his present defeat as final. I shall look forward to a turning in history after the cataclysm is over and the sky is again unburdened and passionless.
>
> — *Ibid.* p. 358-359

Often branded as more a confession than an argument, the voice of Tagore is overpowered by an unusual and shameful approach to Truth by the so-called radicalists. What Tagore wants to emphasize is not to establish a truth by means of a traditional approach to utilitarian arguments which more often than not suffer from political propaganda. Iconoclasm is neither prudence nor sentimentalism but a deep delve into the diverse roots of Truth. The search is inward and not as politicians richly utilize, outward. Tagore remains indifferent to sterile arguments because he is neither interested in being a national leader nor does he find the real avenue of fulness of man in utilitarianism. He is very much misunderstood when his reflections on the suffering humanity as poignantly revealed in unfolding the crisis of civilization are camouflaged by the term confession. Why does he confess, and what ? What is the outcome *sans* beating one's drum for being a messiah ? Tagore never wants to be a messiah. Hs world is the world of fulness of vision in serenity of poignance and perfection. His world is the world of looking within and looking beyond. His prayer is the prayer of inwardness that far exceeds confession and argument. As he muses,

> This is my prayer to thee, my lord—
> strike, strike at the root of penury in my heart.
> Give me the strength lightly to bear my joys and sorrows.
> Give me the strength to make my love fruitful in service.
> Give me the strength never to disown the poor or bend my knees before insolent might.

> Give me the strength to raise my mind high above daily trifles.
> And give me the strength to surrender my strength to thy will with love.
>
> — Rabindranath Tagore : *Gitanjali*, Macmillan India Limited, Macmillan Pocket Tagore, Edition, 1983, No. XXXVI, p. 21.

With the above words of prayer, Tagore believes that the crisis of civilization awaits an inward look. The lost art of seriousness is above bare argument and a reminder to the fallen Eden, the lost paradise to be regained by any means. But before that, let us, as Tagore for the first time exposes with all seriousness and clarity of vision, rise above the misuse of the power of youth and the delirium from which the country terribly suffers :

> To pay part price for a thing may lose both the price and the thing. The daring youths of those days had thought that the sacrifice of their lives on behalf of all the people would bring about a revolution. They paid the highest price in their power but it was not enough. The deliverance of people must spring out of all their hearts, not from the heart of a section. On a railway train a first-class compartment with all its rich fittings cannot go faster than the third-class coaches attached to it. I think that the survivors in that patriotic band have now realized that the country has to be the creation of all its people, a concrete expression of mass mind and will, every faculty pressed into full use.
>
> When we turn our gaze upon the progress of other nations, the political cart-horse comes prominently into view—on it seems to depend wholly the speed of the vehicle. We forget that the cart behind the horse must also be in a fit state

to move; its wheels must have the right alignment, its parts must have been properly assembled. The cart is the product not simply of materials on which saw and hammer had worked; thought, energy and application have gone into its making. We have seen countries that are outwardly free, but as they are drawn by the horse of politics the rattle rouses all the neighbourhood from sleep and the jolting makes the limbs of the passengers ache; the vehicles break down repeatedly on their way and to put them in running order is a terrific business. Yet they are vehicles of a sort, after all. The fragments that pass for our country not only lack cohesion but are composed of parts at odds with one another. To hitch it to anger or avarice or some other passion, drag it along painfully with much din and bustle, and call this political progress ! How long could the driving force last ? Is it not wiser, then, to keep the horse in the stable for the time and rake up the task, first, of putting the vehicle in good shape ?

It appears from the writings of the young men of Bengal who have turned back from the politics of death that such thoughts are troubling their minds too. They say that what we need above all else is self-preparation, a striving to develop the inner man, so that the groundwork for a common endeavour may be ready. This has to be achieved not by blind obedience to an external bidding but by disciplined reason. Whatever fails to illumine the mind and keeps the mind in a state of daze, is a deterrent.

— Rabindranath Tagore : "The Call of Truth", *Towards Universal Man*, Asia Publishing House, Bombay, 1961, p. 259-260.

'A striving to develop the inner man' as Tagore refers to above, is all the more necessary in hours of crisis. Not sentimentalism but discipline in right earnest is the only way to arrest crisis and advance towards national and global efflorescence of inherent goodness in man. Not apeing but creating anew with wider avenues of understanding and appreciation demands greater and more serious attention and endeavour.

The soul of the inner man awaiting the language of emancipation as Tagore thinks, defines the destiny of man. Civilization would proclaim the victory of that inner man's soul out of the crumbling dust of ruins. Let man be allowed to hold his head high in the boundless open sky. Let the unobtrusive sky of belief in man invoke the advent of man the victorious.

Tagore never believes in an evasive ready-made answer to the crisis of crisis—the crisis to bring about a psycho-civilized society. No argument, but a look deep within, work untiringly within, patience within, purity within, promise to safeguard the vision of man serene within are the multi-dimensional avenues of askance with which Tagore alone can present us to ponder over.

> "The enemy is not without but within. Without inwardness we are doomed. No knowledge can be evil, not even the knowledge of evil. But where is the wisdom, the self-restraint that we have lost in the explosion of expertise ? How to be modern as well as man ?
>
> The Sphinx is a Janus. Reason was a helper, reason is the bar. Between a reductive science and what Sri Ramakrishna called the purified will and intelligence (*suddha buddhi*) oh, the difference ! The concentration of the non-human has made us inhuman. That is what Tagore called the killing of the human reality by the imposition

> of the abstract. That could well be a lesson of the crisis.
>
> * * * * *
>
> Caught in that terrible Either/Or, of a collapsing civilization, it is what we do to the crisis rather than what the crisis does to us that will decide the fate of man. Blend of contingency and freedom, atavism and awareness, 'ihaiva' and 'turiya', man's finitude is a witness to his passion for transcendence. Man has first to affirm himself in the universe. That is his first but not his only business. Fragment dreaming of the whole, he has also to evolve and finally to exceed himself, by the emergence of a deeper occult reality."
>
> — Sisirkumar Ghose : 'Crisis of Crisis', *For The Time Being,* Bharatiya Vidya Bhavan, Bombay, 1983, p. 159-166.

To be on the right road to civilization, Tagore prescribes for the spirit of righteousness that alone would serve as an antidote to crisis in civilization. That he earnestly believes in the arrival of a new dawn from the East is primarily due to the fact that in the East alone the past and the future are conquered and reconciled.[1]

As the faith in the West has already 'gone bankrupt', the meeting between the East and the West, a vision Tagore so fondly nursles is shattered. Out of this grim tragedy—the crisis that deeply pains humanity—he awaits the call of righteousness, the call of Truth.[2] Away with ill-feeling in this hour of crisis, 'propitious dawn', as he reminds us with thrilling askance to ponder over :

> Regrettably, we have narrowed down our vision to more material expectations. But even in the West a real concern to rise superior to material interests is now apparent. There I have come across men in

whom the new spirit of renunciation is personified. Those are men who, freed of the petty bonds of nationalism, feel within them the inner oneness of all mankind, and are ready for every sacrifice in working for the fulfilment of the great ideal. I have seen such men in England; they have accepted insult and hurt from the hands of their own people in their struggle to liberate subject races from the tyranny of power. I have seen such renunciation in France too—there is Romain Rolland, for instance, an outcast among his countrymen. I have also seen this in the minor States of Europe. I have watched the faces of students in Europe, radiant with the hope of world unity, and bearing with patience and courage the blows they must suffer for their dream of the glorious age ahead.

In this propitious dawn, are we alone to harp on the faults of others and base our constructive programmes on ill-feelings ? In this new dawn shall we not remember Him, who is one (*Ya ekah*), who is without distinction of colour (*avarnah*) and who with His multiple power makes true provision for the inherent needs of each and every class (*vahudhashakti yogat varnananekam nihitartho dadhati*) ? Shall we not pray to the Giver of wisdom to unite us all in right understanding (*sa no buddhya subhaya samyunantu*) ?

— Rabindranath Tagore : "The Call of Truth", *Towards Universal Man,* Asia Publishing House, Bombay, 1961, p. 272-273.

What an endorsement twenty-one years after the above ! Do we pay heed to the above even now ?

NOTES AND REFERENCES

1. In interpreting the message of Rabindranath Tagore to the

world, Dr. S. Radhakrishnan significantly unfolds Tagore's universal spirit of nationalism that ensures a common heritage of man towards love and conscience, and Indian 'flaming passion of righteousness' :

Rabindranath is a nationalist but not of the wrong type. While he loves his country, he does not hate others. His patriotism is compatible with universal love. While national independence is a phase of social evolution to be necessarily passed through, it is ultimately one to be transcended in the conception of a worldwhole. As each nation embodies some peculiar elements of value necessary for the full expression of Man, the love of a nation as embodying a part of the essence is not incompatible with the love of mankind as a whole. When Rabindranath wants India to build a great future it is not on the national basis. He wants India to attain freedom that she might make her contribution to the world's welfare, that she might be in a position to fulfil her destiny and carry her message through the world. When Rabindranath loves India, it is the love of a soul, of a spiritual principle and not that of land or commerce. He does not want India to struggle for the sake of her national resources, for preserving the integrity of her forests, saving her mines from destruction and keeping the physical wealth of the great country for the use of her posterity. To him this, while necessary, is a low ideal. No doubt it is a great waste from the Indian point of view that India's material resources are exploited by other countries. But this—a few millions more or less—is not a great thing. When the professional politician complains that foreign rule is bad because wealth emigrates, taxation increases, industries diminish, and hundreds of thousands of people perish in famines, it does not appeal to him as forcibly as considerations of soul and culture. The soul of the Indian nation, its ideal, its thought, its conscience, is at stake, the soul with all its aspirations towards the just and the true, with all that constitutes the human being. His point is that national culture dwindles, its soul is subdued, and everything that makes a nation great, faith, purpose, and character, is inevitably melting away. It is the yoke of the mind, the disease of the soul that he points his finger at. We are steadily losing the ancient cultures of India.*** Spiritual powers and resources of India are being wasted; the diviner human powers of feeling and imagination which reach to the inmost depth of being are neither touched nor developed. The way to grow is by keeping the spiritual achievement of the race in the past before the eyes of the present, by preserving the priceless treasures of mind and soul and by incorporating the great spiritual inheritance in the lives of India's present and future citizens. We need to find ways to make available our choicest racial possessions and bringing them to bear upon the lives of the many. It is the spiritual ideal of India that will lend freedom to the human spirit, and break the bonds of narrow and cramping environment. We must war against the rising tendency for the soul to be swallowed up by mere things, that we might get back the sense of communion with the divine.

* * * *

India should have freedom to express her soul with its longing for holiness, its joy of adoration, its fierce spiritual questioning, and its flaming passion for righteousness.

— Dr. S. Radhakrishnan : *The Philosophy of Rabindranath Tagore,* Good Companions Publishers, Baroda, India 1961, p. 177-179.

2. Just a year before writing this treatise, on the occasion of conferring on him the degree of Doctor of Letters, *honoris causa* by the University of Oxford at a Special Convocation held at Santiniketan on August 7, 1940, Tagore speaks on the 'perennial growth of civilization' :

> In an era of mounting anguish and vanishing worth, when disaster is fast overtaking countries and continents with savagery let loose and brutal thirst for possession augmented by science, it may sound merely poetic to speak of any emerging principle of world-wide relationship. But Time's violence, however, immediately threatening, is circumscribed, and we who live beyond it and dwell also in the larger reality of Time, must renew our faith in the perennial growth of civilization towards an ultimate purpose.

INTERPRETING TAGORE'S *JANMADINE* (*ON THE BIRTHDAY*)

Pregnant with rich experiences of life from varied dimensions, Rabindranath Tagore incomparably exposes himself in his *Janmadine.* Already, the promise of such poignance is there in writings prior to this where the look within for a look beyond is at work. Moreover, the zest for life has already been screened with serene and aesthetic modulations. A definite pattern of self-analysis for self-evaluation makes its efflorescence in *Arogya* (*Convalescence*). Self-askance ensures a solid platform in his creative vision. As he categorically observes

> The web of rhythm of words that I have learnt to weave
> Is trapped there
> In the unreachable that averts the eyes of alertness
> In the depth of mind unseen.
> I want to thwart her in name, but name she does not deny.
> If any worth she has,
> Day by day that worth is revealed,
> Passes from hand to hand.
> If with sudden recognition her surprise
> Does entice,

No room she gets in human habitation
For sometime in the shores of the mind she does
remain unkindled
Nursed in confidence
In the disgrace of exposure
In sands does unite day by day.
This weariness is deserted and empty in the world
of hurry,
The gift of the unknown has left something from
age to age
In this great island of the language of literature
Like lifeless coral.

— Rabindranath Tagore : *Arogya (Convalescence) Rabindra-Rachanavali,* Government of West Bengal, Calcutta, 1980, Vol. III, No. 27, p. 837 [Translated by the author.]

The beckoning of the unreachable and the unknown still pulsates the poet. In his conscious being, he visualizes the Time Eternal changing appearance in light and darkness. The language of the original sea of human consciousness reverberates in the form of a message within him, but he finds no meaning of that language. It is a typical trend of consciousness that prompts him like a swimmer to swim along from one shore to the other unendingly. The light and shadow of such a conscious being within him compliment him with a touch of nearness so intense and loving. But then the unreachable makes a definite pattern of efflorescence within him like a painter, and the sense of amazement brings forth a picturesque vision in the mind of the poet. As he adroitly expresses,

In my consciousness
The language of the primal ocean resonates;
Its meanings I know not,
I'm that message.
Only slashing, rollicking

Only tune, dance alone, the screams and noise of pain,
Only this swimming
To ply sometime to this shore, to that sometime
Or sometime in the unseen deep
Sometime on the shores of the legion.
In the swing of the waves of rhythm
What a style of beckoning does emerge and go afloating
With the beckonings of the silent, speechless and motionless
The stream of unending current
Rushes towards the unknown,
Who knows where it ends.
At times light and shade
Bless with the touch by turns
Sometime at a distance, nearby sometime
On the canvas of the course
The Time Eternal takes its two appearances
One after the other
Black and white
Only to the right and to the left are revelation and constraints of revelation
The image of the unreachable in the break of motion
Goes on painting or covering.

— Rabindranath Tagore : *Janmadine*, *Rabindra-Rachanavali*, Government of West Bengal, Calcutta, 1983 Vol. III, No. 9, p. 848. [Translated by the author.]

A serene sense of introspection makes Tagore restless in self-evaluation. The distance between the eternal mystery of the universe and himself makes him entirely mystic. The morning of his birthday is also the morning of a new vision of awakening. It is also the morning to follow the footprints of the distant, for he has already heard the call of the traveller of the distant. Here, too, he is in love with the unknown.

Otherwise, how can he feel the intense nearness of the distant in his heart ? His own destination becomes explicit and visible with all its unreachabilities and the elements of making a traveller of the path *sans* destination and unknown. Here is the poet's exquisite vision :

That day was my birthday
With the salutation of morning
Towards the rising horizon did I feast my eyes
Saw I that the just bathed dawn
Painted the sandal printings of light
On the snowwhite smooth forehead of the mountain.
The great distance in the core of the universe
Became visible to me today in his image
On the throne of the king of mountains.
With great sombreness from age to age
Does it nursle the shadowy deep unknown
Amid the pathless great forest,
And has encompassed the light piercing the distant
Under the impenetrably unreachable
In the circular avenue of rising and setting.
Today on this birthday
The feeling of distance came close to the heart.
Just as the way of that distant star
Amid the nebula and the vapour of light
Is in mystery enveloped,
So in the unreachable did I behold my distance—
A traveller sans *any* destination with the resulting unknown.
Today on this birthday
The footsteps of that very distant traveller did I hear
From the lonely shore of the sea.

—*Ibid.* No. 1, p. 843

[Translated by the author.]

The vision of the sea in forms of diverse imageries becomes a living document of life for Tagore. With the waning of years in his life, a change comes—a change of the nihil where everything finds a new language of identification in simplicity. Not mere attraction or the fascination of sentimentalism soothed and adorned in romanticism but a certain pattern of serenity that makes every object more meaningful and significant to the poet. Perhaps the age of maturity is wedded to the age of serenity where even death finds a new exposure, a new awakening of light. Soaked in the tragic incidents and affairs of life in legion, Tagore finds the point of equivalence between life and death—the great grandeur of the brilliance of eternity. He is now blessed with the vision of that grandeur. The mark of the affluence of light in his life so long imprisoned in the poverty of Providence is in glowing emancipation now. He listens to the drum of time that plays on in light :

> Like clusters of foam
> Restrained in the mighty whirlpool of Time
> This *maya* bedecked with light and darkness,
> The one *sans* body was framed with a physique.
> Know not wherefrom my existence
> From the eternally rushing current
> Did gush forth.
> All of a sudden
> Amid an unthinkable and invisible beginning did it
> create its own centre
> The global existence did peep in the middle
> What a fun is there in the backdrop of this fun
> I know not.
> This play of the endless with the transitory
> Does weave the neglect of the last destruction with
> the new efflorescence
> In light the drum of Time plays on
> The Transitory stealthily comes to encounter in the
> dress of a bride with her
> Adorned with the necklace of
> The jewels of bubbles.
> In the midst of creation does she attain her seat.

The endless proclaims her debut in the horizon of
the end.

—*Ibid.* No. II, p. 850-851
[Translated by the author]

The call of the drum of light has already reached the poet's heart. This has been confessed by him in his earlier poem in *Arogya* where the holy current of conscious course has allowed him to be in unison with the Great in the joyous festival of light :

The touch of joy in the heart of light I receive
Know I that my soul no difference does conceive.
From an ancient lustrous source
In the holy current of conscious course.
Initiated have I been,
On the forehead the mark of victory is given.
It has informed that the source of nectar I know
With the Great I can unite and glow
In this world of wonder
In the avenue of joy I may enter.

— Rabindranath Tagore : *Arogya, Rabindra-Rachanavali,* Government of West Bengal, Calcutta, 1980, Vol. III, No. 32. p. 839

[Translated by the author]

The blessing of light that the poet wants to receive from the Sun is the blessing of consciousness, the blessing that reveals him the truth of the real self embodied in the Soul Eternal. It is the soul that defies death, and the vision of the Light of life beyond death is the only vision with which the elimination of all darkness of life is possible. Life, a great gift of the All Beautiful, is nothing but an entity of newer awakenings, newer dawns of consciousness. What should be the prayer, then, at the fag end of life ? Here is Tagore's prayer :

Let the fortune of carrying on this life
Touch the forehead with eternal blessings,
Like a gift of lustre *sans* beginning
In newer awakenings at every dawn
At the threshold of this longevity on earth.
Let the deep coverings of ematiatedness
Drop day by day
At the door of the divine
Like the night wedded to slumber.
O Sun, manifest your best appearance,
In that divine disclosure
My own soul beyond death do I behold.

— Rabindranath Tagore : *Janmadine*, *Rabindra-Rachanavali*, Government of West Bengal, Calcutta, 1980. Vol. III. No. 23, p. 862.

[Translated by the author]

Does the poet really behold his soul beyond death ? If not, what are the constraints that stand in the way of his vision ? As a lifelong observer of the vast experiences received through manifold reactions with diverse incidents of life, he squarely meets all eventualities and endeavours at filling his vision with a definite spirit of inwardness.

What does Tagore's inward vision reveal about his own self ? How does he expose himself in the light of diverse experiences of life ? An outsider—*Vratya*—and a wayfarer—*pathachari*—as he describes about himself, the home for holding his birth anniversary is everywhere, and like a stream endless and dynamic he goes on from one corner of the globe to the other to accept the hospitality everywhere. In his life he sincerely feels the debts he owes to the East as well as to the West which have filled in his life with the vast treasures of nearness and experience. The mystery of life is unfolded within him with a more buoyant spirit of consciousness. The distant becomes nearer to him with the passage of time and every occasion of birthday becomes meaningful and thrilling with pulsating experiences of global nearness. The doors of hospitality are wide open to him and the message of the world of oneness becomes more living and significant with every occasion of looking within on the auspicious birthday. A living canvas of life as he spreads wide open in front of our eyes becomes an object of awe and wonder :

> Nursled by the river is this life of mine
> The gifts of diverse mountainpeaks
> Flow on its every nerve,
> With different alluvial soil is its field prepared
> The sustenance of life's mystery from diverse dimensions
> Have achieved its furtherance in the abundance of crops
> With manifold webs of the streams of songs of the East and the West
> Its dreams and awakenings are encompassed.
> The river that acts like a messenger of the universe
> And brings the distant nearer
> On the doors of my room does she come with the welcome of the unknown
> My birthday did she celebrate
> For days eternal in her stream
> The moving residence of mine, a captive outside,
> From shore to shore does float on.
> I'm an outsider, a wayfarer am I
> With diverse courses of unbarred hospitality
> My birthday dish is time and again filled *sans* assessment.
>
> —*Ibid.* No. 28

[Translated by the author]

Apart from this vision of inwardness that present us with the majestic union of the East and the West in the form of the stream of life, Tagore becomes a mystic visionary when he considers the very birthday as the symbol of extinction. The living petals of life drop down like falling leaves. The tree of life is aware of its best form of fulness in flowers meant for dedication in the spread of fragrance. Such a dedication in the form of withering away of petals one by one is a happy journey to the land of Death. Death, as it were, waits for unison in the pattern of greetings for the Beautiful. The land to which the flower is unendingly indebted is also rewarded with the profusion of beauty and fragrance. Likewise, the poet looks forward to celebrating the union between life and death on the very birthday. The juncture of life and death will reward him with the exchange of vision between the fatigued day, and the luminous glory that ends in reverence and loveliness. The beyonding of man cannot but endear the world at the time of farewell because there is a touch of nearness, a close sense of affinity coupled with gratefulness to it. The day of birth is one of rejoicings in all serenity and gratitude for the great unison between light and darkness, life and beyonding of life. This mystic vision of life experienced through the imagery of flowers is adroitly depicted as follows :

> One by one from the flower vase
> The petals of roses lean in longevity dropped down
> withering.
> In the world of flowers
> Any deformity of death do I not visualize.
> Towards life ugliness throws not its last irony
> With apathy flowers do not tarnish one
> Indebted to the earth
> The last penury do they return with beauty and
> fragrance.
> The plaintive touch of farewell is there in it,
> No rebuking is there.
> When birthday and the day of farewell encounter
> face to face
> Let me behold in that union
> Betwixt the rising and the setting horizons
> The exchange of the fatigued day—
> The benign and beautiful end illumined glory.
>
> —*Ibid.* No. 26., p. 864
> (Translated by the author]

Earlier, the sense of gratitude that the poet has expressed in his indebtedness to the world of flowers as well as to the world of living beauty for eternity makes us aware of the fact that the mystic vision with which the beyonding of consciousness is blessed makes the poet more introspective with the philosophy of life and death :

> Open the door,
> Make the blue firmament unbarred
> Let the curious fragrance of flowers enter my room,
> Let the first sunshine
>
> Spread o'er the whole body and in every vein
> Thro' the murmuring leaves
> Let me listen to that very message of greetings
> That I am alive
> Let the morning
> Wrap up my mind with its own covering
> As it covers new crops and green fields
> The silent language
> Of love that I've received in my life
> Do I hear in this sky and the air
> With its auspicious invocation do I bathe everyday.
> The truth of the whole life like a necklace of gems
> Do I behold on the breast of the yonder sky.
>
> — Rabindranath Tagore : *Rogashajyay, Rabindra-Rachanavali,* Government of West Bengal, Calcutta, 1983, Vol. III, No. 27, p. 805.
>
> [Translated by the author]

Absorbed with the mystery of beauty as the poet is, he plunges deep down into the mystery of creation. Beyond the horizon of darkness is his vision now awaiting emancipation of an unending aura of consciousness. Truth now emerges in a new form of conviction in Beauty. Together do they contribute to the offerings that are more valuable and beyond the realm of death. The imagery of the sun, too, flashes in the mystery of creation.

A look within in the backdrop of darkness amidst an experience as a witness to the diverse play of creation is the poet's poignant forte. He, then, becomes one with the consciousness of the unexpressed :

> Standing on the edge of the lawn of the play of creation
> Do I behold at times
> The other shore of darkness,
> Where in the endless consciousness of the vast unexpressed I was absorbed
>
> —*Ibid.* No. 13., p. 853
> [Translated by author]

To the sun, the poet has an ardent prayer :

> Today, the words of the saints flash in my mind at dawn
> Remove, O Sun, unfold the covering of light,
> Let me behold amidst innermost halo serene
> The true image of my soul.
> The I that at the end of the day unites the breath of life in the air
> Whose body in ashes would meet its end
> Let it not cast its own shadow on the way of its journey
> In the disguise of Truth.
> In the playground of this earth the taste of the nectar in happiness and sufferings
> Have I, indeed, received at times,
> In the backdrop of the end have I seen the endless again and again.
> And realised that the last meaning of this life was there
> In the image of that beauty
> In that song beyond speech.

When the doors in the playhouse would be wide
open,
My salutation would I leave behind in the shrine of
the earth
And offer those offerings of life
That are priced beyond death.

—*Ibid.*

[Translated by the author]

To prepare a life in the pattern of the invaluable as the poet does so, is to prepare for a living encounter with the world of beyondings. To him, the mystery of life remains no longer a mystery but a serene passport to encounter face to face with the unknown but predictable future. As a foreseer of the future, the canvas of the onward days as he portrays appears living and prophetic :

Yonder the drum plays on,
The turn for change of days came
Amidst the stormy age.
A new and merciless chapter would follow
Otherwise why so much extravagance like this,
The cruel injustice is coming down,
Injustice is brought forth by the very ghost of
injustice,
The messenger of the future.
The turbulent flow of flood that pushes the stones
of miserliness
Sweeps away the barren look of the poor soil.

The accumulated and dead lair of sand
Floats and fills in the openings of extinction,
Springs on the alluvial soil
And thrives grass by continually killing the desert
All the repeated sayings of the old and the sickly
field
Become meaningless like the dumb.
Dead in the heart
One with stored food in the room does not die
outside

The storm of extravagance rushes around them
Breaks apart the shutters of the storehouse, sweeps
away the roof top.
The jolt of accidents swoops on their shoulders
And awakes all o'er the body,
All of a sudden with the signal of unusual death
In the new field the new harvest would bring forth
for cultivation
In the accident the test finale would bring about
To ascertain the accounts of the savings in the
tattered age.
The polished drabness will have to be identified
today
Hence, yonder the drum has played on.

—*Ibid*. No. 16, p. 855-856

[Translated by the author]

The flood of the unexpressed that has encircled the day and the night makes new revelations to the poet on the occasion of his birthday every year. The sunrise of every day is the sunrise of the life that begins anew every year. It is like the portrait by the artist drawn on the canvas, which is yet to be completed. It awaits new fulfilments with the sunrise on every birthday. It is the sunrise of new visions with diversities on the sea-shore of life. As a matter of fact, the waves of the sea of life are always new with every surging movement. Likewise, the poet feels that life regains a newer spurt to thrust ahead with newer promises of perfection. The vast experiences of his life adorned with many birthdays present him with the prize of self-revelation pregnant with exquisite words of self-submission:

In this life of mine woven in the thread of many
birthdays
Did I visualize myself in the assembly of diverse
manifestations.
Once the new year on the breast of the fathomless
sea

Did carry me
With the terrible delirium of waves
Where from horizon to the other
In the vacant sky on the blank firmament
It does deny the shore
On that day did I behold the picture of the world
sans diversity
When with the first line of creation
The sunken future daily traces its own identity
Towards the sunrise.
Looking unendingly on the curtain of waves
Enveloped with the mystery of life, I thought
My life's covering has not yet been opened
The I complete in itself
In secret does remain unknown.
On newer birthdays
The line drawn by the artist with the stroke of the
brush
Fails to expose within it the last identity of a
picture.
Only do I feel
The vast flood of the unexpressed all around
Encircles the day and the night.

— *Ibid.* No. 2, p. 843-844

[Translated by the author]

The yearning for unison with the flood of the unexpressed makes the poet more responsive to the call of the beyonding on birthdays. Every birthday brings forth a new promise, a new awakening, a new consciousness. It is that promise or awakening or consciousness with which he frankly admits that there are many more things in the world that remain unknown and unadorned. The sea of surprise as he rightly feels and admits is the sea of incompleteness. But for that he does not feel desolate. Rather does he firmly believe that posterity awaits the dedicated service of the poet of the future. As a foreseer of humanity, he elicits the vision of man :

In light marvellous

Man visualizes his own exquisite image of the future

On the stage of the world

The turn of gradual efflorescence of consciousness awaits in acts.

In the group of the actors of that drama

Have I dressed myself.

—*Ibid.* No. 5, p. 846.

[Translated by the author]

The vision of man rechristened with the spirit of reawakening also flashes in the mind of the poet. Man reborn with the spirit of freedom becomes the acme of his vision. Tradition takes a new turn among the suffering humanity as he visualizes in his own canvas of the image of the future man. Man, the tortured and dwarfed, will emerge as man the saint and victorious who will take his seat in the meditation of a new creation in passionless manner. The call of that creation is the call of the All Serene awaiting emancipation from the enemy of extinction within oneself.

Let there be as Tagore earnestly advocates, a new history of man—a new history written in a new language of emancipation of man. Let the catastrophe of the resolution of the All Beautiful be in no time averted by man's own rightful and meaningful existence on earth. Let history be written anew with the spirit of safe-guarding humanity.

To be forearmed, as Tagore suggests, with the weapons of self-identity and self-devotion is to be forewarned against the massacre of humanity writ large in wanton destruction and warfare. The real war is not outside but within. Bereft of this truth is to be alien to ourself like a one-winged bird. The spasm of the air indicates that today's man is terribly alone, but not lonely. The twist and turn of every component of consciousness is yet to be felt with stubborn assurance of involvement and accomplishment.

The waiting of the inner man as the poet strongly feels is yet to be heard and appreciated. The beckonings of creativity are, therefore, yet to be responded. The pains of beauty are yet to be felt within. The marauding protest everywhere affects the painter, too, whose brush draws new lines of protest unknown, unheard, uncared. The spring tide of creation surges ahead with foams of reawakening. Who feels ?

The poet cannot remain silent to the call within. He cannot but feel and feel intensely. He cannot but involve himself in the mess of humanity. The burden of ill thoughts heavily works upon him. Disappointments make merriments with cruel destiny. The challenge that the poet accepts is one of bringing about a change in the celebration of consciousness. The lost soul must be revived from the depth of oblivion to the unending flow of life. The odyssey of the journey unknown can be read in the autobiography written in words of candour and simplicity :

> Complex is the world
> Time and again am I entangled at the time of loosening the strings.
> Not easy is the destination
> On the shoulder of the journey unknown do I carry the burden of anxieties
> On the way anywhere and everywhere
> Are hundreds of artificial curves.
> All the time
> Disappointed, the mind at last accepts defeat.
> In the broken rhythm of life unison is lost
> The urge for living lies at the feet of silent dust.
> O the one *sans* hope
> Bring forth on dryness the flood of the life of the universe
> In the vast sky.
> In forests on the grass of the world
> The richly poignant leisure is filled in

At every tree
In the current of the origin of endless peace.
Let that inner mystery in darkness and light
Beckon him right now
In the assembly of the original life in the simple
heavenly muse of the heart
Away with the glory of the soul
That is doled out in the littleness of faded fatigue
Let it be extinct on the abyss of the blob
By dint of the joint conspiracy of the earth and the
heaven.

—*Ibid.* No. 25., p. 863-864

[Translated by the author]

To rise above the sham glory of the soul doled out in littleness, the poet seeks happy refuge in the heart of Nature. The joy in him is the joy that unites sound and colour. The silent clappings of the sky all around is the proof of the power of his joy that makes a happy role of a unifier. Everywhere in Nature the poet feels a sense of nearness that allows him to remain in the midst of the blue of the hill and the horizon. In his own words,

Amidst the blue of the hill and the horizon
The union between the void and the earth takes
place in rhythm and rhyme.
The golden light of the sun of the early autumn
bathes the forest
In the bunch of yellow flowers the blue bee seeks
honey
Betwixt them do I remain
And so all around the sky claps in silence.

— *Ibid.* No. 14. p.

[Translated by the author]

To reach the ripe old age of eighty is to reach the region of poignance. It is also to reach the age of looking anew and looking within in the light of looking back and looking for the future that promises the solemn goal of life in looking beyond. For Tagore, poetry is always a power eternal for cosmic concentration. It is the only means to make a happy marriage between reality and cosmic consciousness. It is also the surest means to unfold the meaning of mystery in the light of unending inner longings.

Like a *dramatis personae,* the poet now is prepared to sincerely play his part in the aura of amazement. A mature poet *par excellence* as he is with an incomparable power of mystic vision, he adroitly makes a serene unison between mystery and meaning.

How does the poet interpret his inner world of mystery at the age of eighty ? The answer is simple but poignant from the point of peerless poetic imagination baked in the delicate but worthy warmth of mystery. The flood-tide of silent Light emerging from a new vision of wonder in him allows him to be swept by the soundless Void of the history of Man. Creation finds a new definition, a new hall-mark of significance. The slime of life, as the poet introspects, rises from the womb of the sea exposing her splendid and secret identity. Man enters the stage of life in the backdrop of such a mystery of creation by means of the gradual unfolding of consciousness. Here is the poet's inner vision vivid, vibrant, pulsating, prophetic and full of the promise for posterity :

> In light marvellous
> Man visualizes his own exquisite image of the future.
> On the stage of the world
> The turn of gradual efflorescence of consciousness awaits in acts,
> In the group of the actors of that drama
> Have I dressed myself.
> I too had the call to lift the curtain
> That is my serene wonder.
>
> — *Ibid.* No. 5, p. 846
> [Translated by the author]

Indeed, the whole poem (poem No. 5) is a magnificent testament of Tagore's theory of evolution in relation to his theory of mystery and wonder.*

The aura of consciousness that the poet feels in his heart of hearts allows him to enter the land of the beyonding of man, where death and life make no difference but are complementary to each other. Sorrow makes a new appearance in the light of consciousness anew. Even when he reaches the fag end of his life he is not embarrassed with the signal of imminent death. Nor even bereavement has any pathetic appeal, for he finds a new revelation of life in the fire of his own bereavement that has burnt himself to be enkindled anew. The mark of victory of life is there in the very setting sun, as it were, of life. Death in such a light of darkness becomes as beautiful as a lovely maiden with a golden countenance. The inseparable relationship between life and death is, therefore, an exposure afresh to fill in the endless light of everlasting glory. In his own poignant experience of the philosophy of life and death, the poet makes an inward journey into the aura of life and death :

> Penetrating the breast of the banquet of birth today
> The news of death of the endearing one has reached
> Bereavement with its own fire has burnt itself
> And became enlightened.

---

* In this poem the Tagorean "Wonder" reaches a new level and intensity, an epic grandeur. A brief and exalted picture of evolution is followed by anticipations of man's further becoming. All this is capped by a final transition which raises the whole to the level of a prayer and an inspired commentary on the nature of wonder stated in the opening lines of the poem.

— Sisirkumar Ghose : *The Later Poems of Tagore,* Sterling Publishers Private Limited, New Delhi, 1989, p. 265.

On the forehead of the evening, the setting sun
adorns
The mark of glory as bright as blood,
Turns the beauty of the countenance of the imminent
night
As lustrous as gold.
Likewise, Death has dressed me with the burning
flame
In the setting end of life.
A life indivisible
Where birth and death are in unison
Makes its appearance.
That glory exposed the hallowed immortality
Engulfed day by day in the poverty of piteous
providence.

— *Ibid.* No. 8 p. 847

[Translated by the author]

Earlier, in *Rogashajyay,* Tagore unfolds the mystery of life and death in the light of this inward vision :

The aura of consciousness
That has hallowed the sky of my heart
Not a captive it is in the narrow bounds of life
Whose beginning is a blob and in whose and death
is meaningless
In the middle, for a while,
The meaning of whate'er is there does it make
resplandent.
All thro' the sky this consciousness prevails
Like the nectar of joy.
Today with the awakening of the morning
This message tunes on in the inmost core of my heart
This message weaves on the sun and the planets and
the stars
With the undisturbed thread of rhythm in the unending
ceremony of creation.

— Rabindranath Tagore : *Rogashajyay, Rabindra-Rachanavali,* Government of West Bengal, Calcutta, 1983, Vol. III, No. 28, p. 806.

[Translated by the author]

The vision of awakening in consciousness as the poet unfolds is one of rich poignance of the ascent of man. The significance of the evening of life is a signal to this ascent. The poet considers the moments of parting with world a journey to the unknown. But the darkness of the evening hours of life presents him with a beautiful imagery. He prepares for his farewell finale to this earth alone but does not feel lonely. The desolate evening is like a lone maiden awaiting his footstep to greet him at the deep dense door of darkness.

The messenger of oblivion is also there to strip off all the dresses the poet owes to the world. Now is the august moment for him to come out of the shell of day-to-day drudgeries of life. The old habits of life are to be renewed in the serene moments of darkness. To be born anew is to renew the role of life, and, that is why it is high time for him at the fag end of life to be emancipated for having an encounter with the new mystery of life. And so the poet makes a new definition of the birthday of his life :

A new birthday do I call one
Whom the evening awakens in light by being baptised in darkness.

— Rabindranath Tagore : *Janmadine, Rabindra-Rachanavali,* Government of West Bengal, Calcutta, 1983, Vol. III., No. 27, p. 865

[Translated by the author]

The hour of a new beginning is a definite lookback to the hour of farewell. The more tender moments with which the poet is gifted on the birthday forces him to make a tender apology. The vision of consciousness is born anew amidst a panorama of diverse experiences of a long life that also admits its indebtedness to annoyance and anxieties. A right balancing of light and darkness, moments of birth and those of farewell to the earth is the avenue of fulfilment for which the poet cannot but shake hands with delicacy.[1] The pressure of change within is the hall-mark of excellence in creative vision and that is the most appropriate strategy for the ascent of man unknown. Let the old world be invited in the ceremony of the ascent of man. How does Tagore observe within himself this ceremony ? How does he respond to 'lack of conviction' to the best ?[2] Here is the orphic voice of the poet full of gracious gratitude to make an enchanting bridge between the present and the past :

> I know you and yet of the yore you are
> Your surroundings, movements, the surging and falling of waves all around
> All of the known world, and yet there is hesitation in the notes of welcome for them
> Away am I from all, the language of your nerves
> Is mine, too ; a sordid wonder do I feel
> When I behold that its touch brings its hesitating identity
> Like the fragile and lean relationship of a foreigner.
> Something do I want to offer, otherwise
> How can life be in unison with life ?
> With footprints uncertain
> I am afraid my bowl is empty, its taste perhaps
> Has lost its former flavour
> Perhaps honour will be at stake in exchange,
> And so, from the distance of fear
> Amidst this loneliness, do I call on you and say,
> The Lady of Life who has adorned me with newer apparels
> To her on the day of separation
> By putting out the ceremonial lamps
> Never bring forth any disgrace in penury of poverty

Strip off all ornaments, one by one with wrappers
sans decoration of colour
Cover yourselves and paint white markings on the
forehead
With fulness of life you also take part
In that function finale, perhaps from the distance
You'll listen to the sounds of the auspicious
conchshell beyond the horizon.

— *Ibid.* No. 29. P. 866
[Translation by the author]

What a serene portrayal in poetic muse !

NOTES AND REFERENCES

1. Illness, gratitude to man and nature, an enlarged vision of the world, the anxiety and annoyance over international anarchy, welcome to the coming poet and to the coming of Man, the moods of reminiscence, and nonsense verse—what a rich close to a life rich in everything! But the question cannot be avoided : to what dark or bright fulfilment is the Lord of Life, his *Jeebandevata* leading the poet ? The first thing that we notice is that he no longer puts the question in the old way. All stylisations are left aside, are felt to be an intrusion, the poetic is nowhere. The obstinate questionings are too real and immediate to permit of frills or tinkerings. Gradually there comes over this poet—lover of man, light and earth—a queer but inescapable feeling of his own separateness, his different destiny. And this, exactly when he wishes to merge himself into the unity. The sense of separateness is, however, something other than egotism, it is more the distance between those who have "gone over" and those who are still here, or, to be more exact, the feelings of one who is between the betwixt. So, if now and then he feels a little "apart" it is not in the manner of callow youth or with the defiance of romantic genius. But, paradoxically, it is the sense of his own uniqueness that seems to bring him near to men and things. The movement of Tagore's sensibility is a delicate

balancing of opposites, and it is not easy to say to which side he leaned more, the here or the hereafter, to man or to the Absolute. *** Tagore's yoga has been in the main unconscious, and now that he is faced with a decision, the hour of leave-taking becomes all the more tender. It is a farewell to all that he has loved and held dear, and the poetry of renunciation is another name for tender apology.

— Sisirkumar Ghose : *The Later Poems of Tagore,* Sterling Publishers Private Limited, New Delhi, 1989, pp. 174-175

2. The ceremony of innocence is drowned; The best lack all conviction, while the worst are full of passionate intensity.

—W.B. Yeats : *The Second Coming.*

INDEX